A NEW KIND OF DREAM DICTIONARY

D0375707

In Your

DREAMS

Falling, Flying, and Other Dream Themes

Gayle Delaney, Ph.D.

HarperSanFrancisco
An Imprint of HarperCollins*Publishers*

Also by Gayle Delaney, Ph.D.

Living Your Dreams

The Dream Kit

Sensual Dreaming:
How to Interpret the Erotic Content of Your Dreams

Breakthrough Dreaming:
How to Tap the Power of Your 24-Hour Mind

New Directions in Dream Interpretation

HarperCollins Web Site: http://www.harpercollins.com
HarperCollins®, ☜®, and HarperSanFrancisco™ are trademarks
of HarperCollins Publishers Inc.

FIRST EDITION

Library of Congress Cataloging-in-Publication Data
Delaney, Gayle M.V.
In your dreams : falling, flying, and other dream themes : a new kind
of dream dictionary / Gayle Delaney. —1st ed.
Includes bibliographical references and index.
ISBN 0–06–251412–1 (pbk.)
1. Dream interpretation. 2. Dreams. I. Title.
BF1091.D3796   1997   154.6'3—dc21   96–36862

98 99 00 01 ❖ RRDH 10 9 8

To my sister extraordinaire, Marcy Delaney Welch, and my father, Bill Delaney, bon vivant, with so much gratitude for all the love, courage, and assistance you have given me over the years.

Contents

Part 2: Dream Elements

Acknowledgments

Adi Lemoine, braveheart! You never flinch, and you have made writing interactive and fun. Thanks for your cheerful, inventive steadfastness in preparing this manuscript and in bringing so much freedom, order, and good humor to my life.

Thank you, Christina Merkley, psychologist-in-training, for your timely help in the research phase.

Caroline Pincus and Tom Grady, thank you for your support and your long view of my dream work. I am delighted to work with you both again and again.

And thank you, Julie Merberg, for having given me the idea to write this book while you were still an editor. And lucky for me that you had turned into an agent by the time I wrote it!

What You Will Find in This Book

My fifth appearance on the *Oprah* show was just over. As usual, I was delighted that Oprah and her producers had created an informative and lively hour teaching millions of Americans how to understand their dreams in a practical, modern, nonsuperstitious way. As I left the stage and the bright lights, I stepped down into the studio's backstage area where, as usual, someone, in this case a handsome young man, rushed up to me and whispered loudly and urgently, "What does it mean when I fly in a dream?" I wanted to help, but the production assistant was hurrying me to the airport. All I could say was, "It's your dream. You created it. Ask yourself what it was like for you to fly in your dream. Was it easy and fun or scary and difficult? Were you showing off, or feeling confident, or about to crash? Ask yourself if that feeling expresses how you feel in your waking life. Your dream is a personalized version of a common dream that describes and clarifies a particular aspect of your current life." Running to the waiting car, I called back to him, "And, for heaven's sake, don't be satisfied with a standard interpretation of flying that you get from a psychologist or dream dictionary!"

At the top of the list of almost everyone's curiosity about dreams is the question "What do my common dreams mean?" In my twenty years of writing and talking about dreams all over the world in universities, on more than five hundred television shows, and on thousands of radio shows, journalists, students, professionals, and audience dreamers all want to know what their dreams of flying and of falling and of taking impossible examinations mean. No matter how sophisticated a magazine article is intended to be, the journalist always has to include at least a sidebar on common dreams and their meaning. No matter how arrogant a scientist who believes that dreams have no meaning, he or she always breaks down and asks me what a certain common, recurring dream might mean. *In Your Dreams* answers that almost irresistible urge to understand common and recurring dreams while it provides a personalized, intelligent, and practical method for finding one's own personal dream meanings. Here you will find a way to interpret your dreams that honors the very personal versions and meanings of even the most common dreams you have at any given moment in your life.

The first book most people buy on dreaming is usually a dream dictionary. After reading one or two pages, dreamers are generally disheartened to find silly, ridiculous, or just plain far-fetched interpretations, and they often give up on dream interpretation. After all, it takes only a minute to recognize that a dream about a Harley Davidson motorcycle may mean something entirely different to a dreamer who is a Hell's Angel than to one whose son was killed on such a cycle or to one whose husband just bought her a Harley for her fortieth birthday or to a dreamer so poor that she could never hope to buy one. Not to mention how the meaning would change if the dream machine were stolen, damaged, or out of gas! Intelligent bookstore owners know that dictionaries that provide fixed, often superstitious, meanings for dream images are useless. But they feel they must carry them because their customers demand them.

All of us are naturally curious about the odd, puzzling, sometimes delightful, sometimes terrifying stories that come from our brains in sleep. We are attracted by dictionaries because they seem to offer accessible, straightforward answers to our questions. But I don't believe in one-size-fits-all dream meanings. And after reading just a few pages in this book, neither will you.

We all want straightforward answers to the puzzles of our dreams. Yet we know that an interpretation that fails to take into account the particular conditions of our lives and personalities and the particular details of our dream can never be accurate.

This is why I have written a new kind of dictionary— one that, like the old-fashioned kind, lets you go straight to the theme or image you are curious about. But unlike those rigid books, this dictionary will show you how to discover the very personal meaning of your dream in an engaging, interactive, and informative way.

Each entry dealing with a common dream theme, dream animal, person, setting, and object is divided into four sections:

1. *Variations:* Here you will read frequently occurring versions of the theme or image.

2. *What Others Have Said:* Here I highlight interpretations offered by dream analysts such as Sigmund Freud; Carl Jung; Medard Boss; Ann Faraday; my colleague, Loma Flowers; and myself. I have included, here and there, interpretations made by Artemidorus from Asia Minor, who wrote a dictionary in 200 C.E. that has been the secret source for many modern and inflexible dream dictionaries. Some of his interpretations will get you thinking; some will just make you laugh.

3. *Sample Dreams:* Here you will find usually two dreams and their interpretations drawn from the files of my students' and clients' dreams. These examples will show you how real-life dreamers found their personal meanings by using the questions listed in section four of each entry. I have collected thousands of dreams over twenty years from people who came from all over the world to study with us at our dream center in San Francisco. Our dreamers include not only mental health professionals but also professionals and nonprofessionals in almost every field from mothering to law, nursing, the arts and sciences, and business. A few examples come from distant clients I have talked with regularly by telephone and have met but once or twice in person. I have worked with some clients in French and some in Italian. Their ages range from nine to eighty-five.

4. *What Do You Say?:* Here you will find the key questions that will help you uncover the very personal meanings in your dreams. These questions are part of the Dream Interview method of interpretation, which I developed to liberate us from the spell of doctrinaire interpretive theo-

ries of the past. These questions will guide you, first, to describe and explore, then to connect your dream images to real, current issues in your daily life.

Together the sample dreams and the Dream Interview questions will give you a healthy respect for the individual nature of your common dreams—why you dream them on a particular night and not another. They will show you how to put your dream images into the dramatic context of your whole dream and how to put the meaning of your dream into the context of your whole life. When we sleep we do some of our most creative, least defensive, and most insightful thinking. We throw away any chance of benefiting from our night's mental work if we accept prefabricated, arbitrary meanings and if we fail to see how a particular dream sheds light on our current concerns.

You create your dreams every night to deal with the concerns of your day. You use images and themes drawn from your life experience to make metaphors or parables that express how you really feel and what you really think about your life as seen from your sleeping mind's perspective. This book will help you appreciate and put to good use the very careful, custom-tailored work you do for yourself every single night.

Why Common and Recurring Dreams Are Important

We all dream of being chased, of falling, of flying, and of making love to surprise partners, but most of us never know why. The common interpretations we look up in old-fashioned dream dictionaries never satisfy our curiosity because they cannot take into account the specific concerns and circumstances of our private lives. Yet deep down we know our dreams must mean something, and when we dream the same dream more than once, we can't help but think that our sleeping mind is trying to tell us something important. In fact, recurring dreams signal recurring situations and often indicate that we are stuck in a rut in our personal or work life. As humans on one planet, we all share a great number of hopes and fears. We fear falling, and we love to fly. We hate to miss a train, and we love to find money. But why do we all dream similar dreams on different nights? And why are there such important differences between our version of a common dream and someone else's? Learning why we dream a common dream at a particular time in our lives can open the door to new insights that will help us understand ourselves and get out of the ruts that keep us from maturing and living fuller, happier lives. In most cases, our common dreams represent a recurring theme or problem in our lives. Often this theme is one we share with many other people. By understanding our particular version of a common dream, we can resolve a recurring problem and at the same time appreciate the fact that many of us at one time or another share similar difficulties in living.

For two decades as a television and radio guest expert on dreaming, I have been telling people to *throw away* those simplistic dream dictionaries most of us at one point in our lives have been fooled into buying. I have written this book on common dream themes to provide you with material that respects your individuality and the unique circumstances of your life. Here are the tools to uncover the personal, practical insights your common but personalized dreams contain.

How to Recall Your Dreams More Vividly

Even if you almost never remember your dreams, you can learn to recall them regularly and vividly within one or two weeks using simple steps that have worked without exception for thousands of my clients over the past twenty years. Try these simple steps and you will see.

1. Keep a notepad beside your bed.
2. Before going to sleep tonight, jot down the date and three or four lines about what you did and felt today.
3. As soon as you awake, before getting out of bed, write down whatever is on your mind. Learn to think backward the minute you awake. Ask yourself, "What was just going through my mind?"

Jot down anything that comes to mind—a little piece of a dream, one solitary image or feeling, or just the fact that your mind seemed blank and that you are frustrated not to have caught a dream. By writing down just a line or two each day, you will teach yourself to notice what is in your mind upon awakening. And since we almost always are dreaming just before we awake, soon you will be able to remember plenty of dreams.

Don't worry about remembering a dream every day. If you remember one or two dreams a week you will have plenty to keep you busy as you begin working with your dreams.

If you can get a full eight hours of sleep, avoid drugs and alcohol, and awake without an alarm clock, you will greatly enhance your dream recall.

Guidelines for Interpreting Your Dreams

No more silly fixed interpretations, no elaborate and esoteric psychological theories from the first half of the century. I will teach you how to interview yourself (or a fellow dreamer) so that you can discover the very personal meanings within your wildest, funniest, weirdest, saddest, or most haunting dreams.

DREAM DIAGRAMMING

When you are just beginning to use the Dream Interview method, having a copy of the dream in front of you will make it easier for you to mark out or diagram its elements. Here is how we do it at the Delaney & Flowers Dream Center:

1. *Settings:* Draw a rectangle around the words indicating the setting of any particular scene.

2. *People and Animals:* Circle the main characters.

3. *Objects:* Underline the major objects.

4. *Feelings:* Draw a wavy line or circle around any words that describe or suggest feelings. If none or very few appear, be sure to ask about feelings and jot them down as you go through the interview.

5. *Action:* Underline with an arrow the major actions in the dream.

Here is a sample dream diagrammed:
I was in the house I used to live in with my first husband. It was cold and dark. I was anxious and uncomfortable.

My friend (Laura) came into the living room where my (husband) and I were sitting on the couch. She sat down between us and showed us a plate of burned food that she had cooked. She was crying and said that she couldn't do anything right. I felt very sorry for her because she was so sad and depressed.

Once a dream is diagrammed, you will be able to identify the type of dream element you are dealing with, and you can use the Dream Interview questions tailored to that element to discover what the image means to you in a particular dream.

The Dream Interview Method

Working with your own or a friend's dream is a fascinating undertaking, but it can be a frustrating one without guidelines. The whole idea behind using this method is to focus efficiently on the personal meanings a dream image has for the dreamer. At our dream center we set up an interview situation in which the interviewer and dreamer pretend that the interviewer comes from another galaxy and is unfamiliar with life on earth. This allows the interviewer to keep an open mind and to ask questions that help the dreamer find his or her own meanings without unnecessary suggestions and projections from the interviewer. Following the six basic interview steps in a flexible but thorough way will help you interpret any dream. These steps work with both your most common and your most bizarre dream adventures. If you are working alone, as most people are, you can play the roles of both the dreamer and the dream interviewer. If you are working with a friend, take turns interviewing each other.

1. *Get a definitive description* of all the major dream elements. Ask the dreamer to describe and, in the case of objects, to define the major elements of the dream as if she were describing them to someone from another planet who depends on her to learn about life on earth. Be sure she includes her feelings or judgments about each element. For example, "What is a car like? How do you like cars?" or "What is a car? Why do humans use them, and what is the one in your dream like?"

2. *Restate or recapitulate* each description using the dreamer's words and tone. Do not add your own words or associations if you are interviewing a partner. When you work alone, it might help especially in the beginning of your study to jot down your description and then review it to be sure it is complete. The particular words the dreamer chooses usually trigger the dreamer's recognition of the meaning of an image or theme. Edit and synthesize slightly if necessary to get to the core of the description. Do not interpret, just reflect the dreamer's descriptions.

3. *Bridge* from the dream images to specific situations in the dreamer's or your own life. Ask, "Does (restate the description) remind you of anything or anyone in your life?" Or, "Does it remind you of any part of yourself?" You may want to bridge each image as you go along or wait until you have described several images. This step is one of interpretation and should be taken only after you have elicited and restated a rich description. Remember: Describe before you interpret!

4. *Test* the strength of the bridge. Verify and clarify. Have the dreamer tell you specifically *how* the dream element relates to her waking life. Say something like, "You say this dream image (or action or feeling) reminds you of *x*. How so?" Be sure there is a good match between the

dream image and the life issue to which the dreamer has connected it. If you discover that the bridge is weak, return to the description step again or go on to the next images and gather more clues before circling back for another, more complete description. Then, armed with more information, try to bridge again.

5. *Summarize* the descriptions and bridges as you go along, especially at the end of each scene and at the end of the interview. Ask the dreamer to correct you if you misstate or give an inappropriate emphasis to any part of the summary. Invite the dreamer, or feel free if you are the dreamer, to add any thoughts that occur as you are making your summary. It is during this step that many dreamers start to recognize the meaning of their dreams. As the dreamer listens to a summary or conducts one for himself, the pieces of the dream continue to fall into place, and the overall meaning of the dream usually comes to light.

6. *Reflect:* Invite the dreamer (or yourself) to consider what, if any, actions or changes in attitude might be appropriate given what she has (or you have) learned from the dream interview. Ask the dreamer to reread the dream two or three times over the next week and to make a point of keeping in mind the major dream images and insights for the entire week. Writing a one-page summary of the dream interview will help you understand and remember your insights even better. My book *Breakthrough Dreaming* describes this Dream Interview method in great detail. You can order it at any bookstore if you want more instruction.

Don't be intimidated by your dreams. If you take one image at a time and fully describe it using the questions listed for each theme or image, you will teach yourself, over time, to make good interpretations. You are learning a new language—one of pictures, feeling, and metaphor. With practice you will be able to go from understanding single images to interpreting short, easy dreams to understanding longer, more difficult ones. All along the way, new perceptions and insights will open up to you.

PART 1

Dream Themes

1 Theme & Variations

How to Interpret Any Theme in Your Dreams

Almost every dream has a theme, which may be common or uncommon. Without understanding the theme, you will usually be at a loss to make sense of the individual images—the people and things you dream up. This first entry is dedicated to helping you figure out any theme you conjure up. The rest of the entries will deal with the most common dream themes and will serve as models you can use to modify your interview for any theme.

Try using the interview questions listed below to explore the meaning of any theme not listed in this book. They will help you follow the basic interview steps of:

1. Getting a good description,
2. Recapping that description, and
3. Bridging or connecting the image described to something in your life.

Remember, pretending that the interviewer comes from a different planet will help you give concise answers that get to the point about what you really feel and think about the images in your dream. This will work whether you give the role of interviewer to a partner or play it yourself. These questions should provide you with the material to connect your dream experience to your waking experience and thus to interpret your dream according to your own meaning system. This, after all, is the one you went to sleep with before you created the dream. Good luck!

1. *Describe* the main theme in your dream. Are you being suffocated? Are you being chased by someone? Have you lost your purse? Do you find yourself naked in public? How do you feel in the dream? Describe feelings and attitudes very specifically. Remember, your interviewer comes from another planet and doesn't know how a human like you would feel in such a situation. Can you find three adjectives to describe your experience? So in your dream (restate briefly the description and see if the dreamer concurs with your recapitulation).

2. Is there any situation in your life in which you have the same feelings you just described? (Bridge) How so? Can you tell me more specifically how they match? (Testing the bridge.)

3. How might this dream theme shed light on your deepest and most honest feelings, your hopes, your fears, your concerns in your waking life? (This question will help the dreamer to summarize and reflect upon her dream.)

Being Chased

VARIATIONS

Being chased in a dream is usually frightening. We are chased by all kinds of people, animals, and sometimes elements like storms, lightning, and thunder. Often dreamers do not remember much detail, only that they were trying to escape from a mean beast or a huge bug or a threatening man. The pursuer might carry a gun or a knife or might simply exude a sense of ominous threat. Dreamers almost always awaken before they are caught. Some, however, manage to outwit their pursuers before awakening. In some cases the dreamer is caught by the pursuer, and in some the dreamer decides to stop running, turns around, and asks the assailant, "What do you want? What are you doing in my dream?" At this point any number of surprises may occur.

WHAT OTHERS HAVE SAID

Many psychoanalysts, following Freud, have interpreted the dream of being chased as the disguised form of the wish to be captured and to have a sexual encounter. Jungians often suggest to their dreamers that the pursuer represents a disowned part of the dreamer's personality that may need to be accepted and incorporated rather than rejected and run away from. At the dream center, before offering even a hypothetical interpretation, we ask the dreamer to describe what he or she is running from and what the main feelings are in the dream—both the feelings of the dreamer and the perceived attitudes and intent of the pursuer. Approaching the dream this way allows a tremendous variety of interpretations, because, as should be no surprise to any of us, we all have a habit of running away from a great variety of people, situations, and fears that we find intolerable.

Sometimes the dreamer will use a chase dream to describe how he is running away from a part of himself that he refuses to recognize. Or a young girl might be running away repetitively from an older, powerful, threatening man who reminds her of her aggressive and abusive father. Others dream of running away from animals that remind them of aggressive parts of their own personality or of someone in their family or someone at work. People run away from indistinct images that are dark and threatening and that may represent aging, death, or poverty. We run away from our fears. In so doing, we are bound to dream of being chased by something threatening. The things that chase us in the night may simply represent our own fears and fearfulness in living.

Getting a precise description of whatever is chasing you will help you discover what you are avoiding in your life at this particular time. Usually only *after* you interpret your dream will you see that you have been running away; before the dream work you may not even have known that a problem was creeping up on you. When the insight hits and you realize just what you are avoiding in your life, you will recognize that you are way ahead of yourself while dreaming.

SAMPLE DREAMS

Chased by Thug

Joseph dreamt regularly of a contemporary thirty-year-old male thug who was running after him, trying to get him. Sometimes the thug had a gun, sometimes a knife, sometimes just his bare hands. Joseph would awake with his heart pounding, full of anxiety.

This is a very common version of a chase dream. When Joseph described the thug in his dream as a rough, uncouth, inconsiderate oaf who was very self-centered and unconcerned about the needs of others, he saw a parallel to himself. He saw the part of himself that had yet to be civilized and that drank too much, that drove while drunk, and that could be extremely hostile toward people who angered him. In the dream he felt threatened by this aspect of his personality, which was threatening his career and his relationship.

Chased by Men with Knives

Elena dreamt the following dream perhaps three times a year over the period of more than a decade: "I was walking down a street in the city. It was night, and two young men brandishing knives were chasing me. I woke up terrified."

This is a common dream in which women feel threatened by men carrying guns or knives. Often the dreamer can't say much about the pursuers, only that they are threatening. It is not clear what they want to do to the dreamer, perhaps kill her, but their ill intent leaves the dreamer feeling terrified. In this case Elena said that the feelings in the dream described her feeling of vulnerability in the urban environment she lives in as well as her feeling of being threatened more generally by a variety of situations in which she feels unprotected and alone.

WHAT DO YOU SAY?

1. Describe, being as specific as you can, just how you feel as you are being chased in the dream.

2. Can you say why this person is chasing you and what is his or her intent?

3. What is the person or thing like that is chasing you?

4. Does this, which you describe as (restate the description), remind you of anything or anyone in your life that you are running away from or that seems to be after you?

5. Do the feelings you experience in the dream remind you of any situation in your life?

6. Instead of fleeing, what would be a better way of dealing with the conflict or the problem?

Teeth Falling Out

VARIATIONS

While many common dreams come in both pleasant and unpleasant versions, a dream of having your teeth fall out seems always to give the dreamer an awful feeling. The good news is that if you can figure out why you are having your particular version of this dream at this particular time in your life, you may be able to understand something important about your life and resolve a conflict or two.

Almost everyone has dreamt of teeth falling out. Sometimes people dream that their teeth are crumbling into their hands or, worse yet, that they can feel the teeth totally loose like stones inside their mouths. Some dreamers say that it is just at the point of smiling that their teeth spurt out of their mouths. Almost everyone feels either shocked or embarrassed.

WHAT OTHERS HAVE SAID

Throughout the ages, almost everyone has had something to say about the dream of losing teeth. The Chester Beatty papyrus, which dates from 2000 B.C.E., tells us that a dream of teeth falling out foretells death at the hands of one's dependents. In the Talmud we are told that these dreams mean the death of some member of the dreamer's family.

In 200 C.E. Artemidorus, an extremely well-traveled and well-read writer on oneirocriticism, or dream interpretation, published a book surveying much of the literature and oral tradition in Asia Minor, Greece, and Rome at that time. In his book Artemidorus wrote, "The upper teeth represent the more important and excellent members of the dreamer's household; the lower, those who are less important." He goes on to explain that losing one's teeth foretells the loss of more or less important people or possessions. If the dreamer is healthy, free, and not a merchant, it could mean that his house will be deserted by everyone. "If a slave dreams that he has no teeth, it signifies his freedom." If the dreamer is sick, the indication is "lingering illness, but it clearly signifies that no death will result."[1]

Like most people before him, Artemidorus believed that almost all dreams foretell the future. This led to some creative soothsaying with interpretations that never had to stand the test of scientific surveys or experiments. Artemidorus did, however, have an extraordinary grasp of metaphor and of how the meaning of a dream depended upon the circumstances and culture of the dreamer. If he had not been so bent upon extracting a prediction out of every dream, his skills with metaphors might be very useful to us eighteen hundred years later.

Freud read Artemidorus yet failed to adequately appreciate the personal qualities of dream metaphors. He suggested instead his usual interpretations along the lines of sexuality and repression. If a young woman dreams of teeth falling out, it expresses her perhaps unconscious wish to have children, since there is something coming out of her body. Teeth falling out for a man may express his anxiety and fear of castration. Here the teeth are interpreted as a symbol that camouflages the hidden dream thought of the penis.

Ernest Jones, a modern Freudian, and a young Carl Jung concurred with this view.

More recently, I have heard Jungians and New Age interpreters suggest the dream of teeth falling out signifies a fear of aging or a loss of one's power and aggressive faculties (the ability to bite). However, I have never seen this commonsense explanation to be relevant to the dreamers I have worked with.

The existentialist psychoanalyst Medard Boss interpreted these dreams as reflecting the dreamer's anxiety at the loss of one's old way of seeing or grasping the world. Then, of course, there are those who believe that a literal interpretation is always to be considered and that the dreamer should have a dental checkup!

At our dream center the above interpretations have not surfaced. What I have commonly noticed is that if we take the time to ask the dreamers how they feel in the dream about losing their teeth, they say they fear "looking bad" or losing face. When we ask if there is any waking situation that might give rise to such concerns, they can usually point to a recent time when they feared not looking pretty enough or having lost face after having said or done something they later regretted.

SAMPLE DREAMS

Teeth Crumble

Claudio dreamt: "I was sitting with a group of friends when I suddenly felt all my teeth crumble in my mouth. I knew that as soon as I opened my mouth they would all fall out."

Claudio asked himself if the feelings of anxiety and imminent embarrassment that he felt in the dream reminded him of any recent life situation. Sure enough, the dream seemed to be exaggerating his situation at work. He dreamt this dream the night after his first meeting as the new manager in his office. He interpreted the dream as pointing out to him that he was not as confident as he pretended to be—that, in fact, he was terribly worried that he had been prematurely promoted. He felt he would say something so stupid that all would know he was too inexperienced for the post. The dream helped him recognize and work with his anxiety.

Teeth in Hand

Katherine dreamt: "My teeth suddenly fell out into my hand. All of them!"

When she asked herself exactly how she had felt in the dream and why this situation might lead to such feelings, Katherine found the meaning of her dream. Katherine was in the process of getting a divorce after twenty years of marriage. The dream feelings of dreading having to be seen toothless and old vividly depicted her worst fears as she reentered the singles' world. She knew that she had better come to terms with the realities of being fifty and single if she was to date with any self-confidence, a quality that attracts potential mates.

WHAT DO YOU SAY?

Now it's your turn. Here are some Dream Interview questions that will help you find out why you dreamt of your teeth falling out right at this time.

1. Why would a human like you (remember, I come from another planet) care if his or her teeth fell out? In other words, what's wrong with having your teeth fall out?

2. If you know, describe which teeth fell out and how it came to happen.

3. How do you feel in the dream about all this?

4. Do the feelings you have in your dream remind you of any feelings or of a recent situation in your life?

5. How so? Check to see if you have made a good match or bridge between your dream and your life feelings. If not, describe your dream feelings more fully until you see the parallels in your life.

Being Naked in Public

VARIATIONS

We are sometimes totally naked and sometimes only partially undressed, but in all these dreams of being naked in public we feel embarrassed, ashamed, and, oddly, usually incapable of making an exit or finding some clothing. Another strange thing about these dreams is that usually the people who see us don't care. They seem indifferent to both our nakedness and our suffering. Sometimes we know the people who are looking at us; they might be friends or family members. This dream almost always seems to end badly, in more or less frozen embarrassment, and we wake up feeling wretched. Only rarely do dreamers tell of not being embarrassed and of actually finding an unexpected comfort in nakedness.

WHAT OTHERS HAVE SAID

Freud considered naked-in-public dreams to be exhibition dreams. He saw them as expressing the hidden wish to be noticed, although this wish is censored and in the dream is represented by the indifferent strangers. Freud also thought that these dreams could represent historical moments in the dreamer's life when as a child the dreamer exhibited himself to his friends and perhaps was very embarrassed by their reaction or by the reaction of parents who caught him in the act. Freud also thought dreams of nudity might reflect actual memories of being examined by doctors in medical situations where indifferent people were looking at one's naked body; the patient might or might not have felt embarrassed about his body, but he did have a wish to be noticed and to expose himself. Or, Freud thought that these dreams could express wishes to return to our earliest childhood sense of freedom and lack of conflict in showing our physical selves to the world in playfulness. Freud believed that dreams of being naked in public contained the fulfillment of a wish based on infantile exhibitionistic tendencies, which every child has. This desire is thought to be repressed from childhood on and finds its expression in the dream state. Other psychoanalysts, such as Emil Gutheil, who wrote about dreams in the 1950s, thought that this dream can also express the dreamer's feelings of guilt or of inferiority—that in the naked state the dreamer shows his shortcomings, can be easily criticized by others, and thus has reason to be ashamed of himself.

My colleague, Dr. Flowers, and I have noticed that these dreams tend to express not a wish but an anxiety and a worry about feeling overexposed, feeling terribly vulnerable, and feeling that you'll be criticized and not have any defenses at your disposal. The indifference of the onlookers, most dreamers tell us, makes them think that their concern about being overexposed is exaggerated and that the rest of the world doesn't really notice their sense of vulnerability or nakedness. Every once in a blue moon I hear a dreamer tell me that she was naked in a dream and at first was very embarrassed but then realized it didn't really matter and woke up feeling just fine. These dreams can signal a growing sense of the dreamer's comfort with her body and perhaps with her sexuality.

SAMPLE DREAMS

Emilio in the Streets

Emilio dreamt that he was standing in the middle of a busy street in Rome (his home) among four lanes of traffic when he suddenly realized he was naked from the waist down. He felt very awkward and didn't know what to do.

When I asked him how he felt being naked in the middle of a Roman street he said, "Well, I was embarrassed." I asked, "Why were you embarrassed?" He responded, "Well, the cars go very fast, the drivers are very aggressive, and I felt very vulnerable." He was then able to bridge the dream feelings to those he was having in his waking life in his new job, where he was surrounded by very aggressive people and needed to learn how to gird his loins for his professional battles.

In the Green Bathtub

Susanna dreamt that she was attending a beautiful party at a posh ski resort in Switzerland. She was in a spectacular private home, and everyone was dancing and having a good time on the first floor. She decided to go upstairs and take a bath in her hostess's luxurious bathroom. The bathtub was emerald green, about ten feet by ten feet square and about four feet deep. She slipped into the tub as beautiful music was playing. She was happy just to relax and soak in the tub, but then she noticed that other people were walking by the bathroom and the door was wide open. At first she was embarrassed, thinking she should get out of the warm tub, close the door, and make sure no one could see her. But then she thought, "Ah, it's no big deal, I don't care if they see me. I am having such a wonderful time."

Susanna described her feelings in the dream and realized that they perfectly paralleled her growing sense of confidence in her own sensuality and her ability to go after what she wants in life. She was surprised that in the dream she was able to stop worrying about being seen, which reminded her of her own determination to become more comfortable both in public and in private with her sensual, sexual side.

WHAT DO YOU SAY?

1. Describe the setting in which you are naked.
2. How do you feel being naked in this setting? Remember, I come from another planet and have no idea how humans feel in such situations.
3. Is there any situation in your current life in which you feel as you do in the dream, for example, overexposed or vulnerable?

4. In the dream, does anyone else care that you are naked?

5. If no one else in the dream cares that you are so exposed, could it be that in your waking life you are overly concerned with being vulnerable or feeling emotionally exposed?

6. Do the feelings and situations in the dream remind you of any situation in your recent or past waking life?

7. How so?

8. Is there anything you could do to relieve your anxiety (such as discussing it with a friend or therapist)?

Cars You Drive

VARIATIONS

Car dreams are very common and often extremely powerful. We may dream about finding a car we thought we had lost or of realizing we own a car we never knew we owned. We may dream about suddenly driving down the road in a very unusual car of a particular year or a particular color. Sometimes our dream cars are having mechanical difficulties. Sometimes we carry passengers we don't like or passengers who cause us trouble. Or we may dream of driving recklessly or being out of control. Sometimes we dream of being afraid to test the power of a car we own. Other times we dream of driving someone else's car; we might be driving our mother's car or the car of our employer or the car of a friend or lover.

WHAT OTHERS HAVE SAID

Carl Jung wrote that to see a car in a dream illustrates the way the dreamer moves forward in time, how he lives his psychological life. A borrowed car might illustrate that the dreamer is living in someone else's psychological or personality style rather than in his own. Freud suggested that a car could symbolize the dreamer's body ego. The headlights could be the eyes, the motor could be the sexual organs or vital organs, the fenders the extremities, the trunk of the car the back, lower bowel, rectum, or anus, and the gear shift and steering wheel could refer to the male genitals!

My colleague, Loma Flowers, and I, along with psychoanalyst Alexander Grinstein, have noted that the year, the make, and the condition of the car often symbolize a particular time in the dreamer's life in which certain emotionally charged events occurred. These characteristics can suggest a mood, personality style, or a way of being in the world. In some dreams the dreamer has a difficult time getting the car started or finds that the tires have been slashed or that the clutch won't engage or that the car keeps stalling out, suggesting the dreamer's trouble getting going in life.

SAMPLE DREAMS
The Highly Chromed Car

George dreamt that he was driving a 1950s Corvette that was extremely rare and highly overdecorated. The mirrors were very big, and the chrome was extraordinarily shiny and exaggerated all over the car.

George said that only a real show-off would drive such a car. As we interviewed him about the dream, he realized he had created a dream picture of himself and of his exaggerated need to show off and look smart. He desperately wanted to be cool because in waking life he was trying to compensate for a deep sense of inadequacy that he had carried with him since childhood. The dream helped him see that as an adult he acted a bit silly from time to time, showing off in a way that really was not very cool.

The Ferrari in the Garage

Jeannette dreamt that she walked into her garage and discovered a beautiful red Ferrari, the hottest, sexiest car she had ever seen. Then she realized that the car had been sitting in her garage for years and that she had never known it. The keys were in her hand, so she got into the car and took it for a ride. Suddenly she realized she didn't know how to work the brakes, so she slowed down and decided to take the car to a mechanic to find out how to operate them.

When she interviewed herself regarding this dream, Jeannette described this Ferrari as extremely powerful, extremely agile, sexy, and extraordinarily flamboyant. She was delighted to have such a car, and she bridged the description of the car to her own sense of power and excitement in life, which she had greatly underestimated until very recently.

Describing brakes, she said they are very important because you mustn't go fast if you don't know how to stop, or you'll kill yourself. She bridged the problem with the brakes to her own difficulty in harnessing her new energy and her sense of power so that it would enrich her life rather than endanger her well-being by being used recklessly.

Linda's Heap

Linda dreamt that she was driving through town in a battered old jalopy. She pulled into a parking lot, got out of her car, and, looking back at her car for the first time, realized how awful it looked next to all the other cars. When Linda described the car in her dream and how she felt about it, she realized she was describing her own attitude toward herself and her body. She really was treating herself like a jalopy. She had neglected taking care of her body. She never dressed up anymore and rarely looked in the mirror. This dream motivated her to join a health club, get a new wardrobe, and start thinking about herself as someone who doesn't have to go through the world looking like an old jalopy.

Driving My Wife's Car

Winston dreamt that he was driving his wife's car when it broke down. He tried to fix it but just couldn't figure out what to do. Finally he discovered that if he fiddled around with the electrical circuitry he could connect things up so the car would run beautifully.

When I asked him to describe the car in the dream, he said it was his wife's and that electrical connections seemed out of whack. At this point he started to laugh and said, "You know, that sounds like my wife. Emotionally she is very confusing to me. I haven't learned to talk about feelings the way she has, and I have worried that she might leave me and that I might be stranded because I haven't been able to meet some of her emotional needs. Part of the solution is just talking about my own emotions. So in the dream I put a lot of effort into it, and I was very happy when I was successful in making the right connections. I really would like to have a more intimate relationship with my wife."

WHAT DO YOU SAY?

1. Describe the car in your dream.
2. What make and what year is the car? How is the car working in your dream? What is the feeling of driving this car?
3. How would you describe the personality of such a car?
4. Does this car which you describe as (restate the description) remind you of any part of yourself or of anyone in your life or of any situation or feeling that is familiar to you?
5. How so?
6. Does the dream situation remind you of any current life circumstances?
7. How so?
8. Is there anything you would like to do about it?

Cars Driven by Others

VARIATIONS

We dream of being not the driver but the passenger in a car. Sometimes the driver is capable, and sometimes the driver is distracted or reckless. Sometimes we sit in the front seat, sometimes in the back seat. Frequently, bad things happen in a dream that begins with somebody else driving the car we are in. In other versions we see known or unknown people driving a car that may or may not be our own, a car that may be unfamiliar or familiar. The type of car and the condition of the car are important and, of course, can vary widely from one dream to another.

WHAT OTHERS HAVE SAID

In addition to the comments in the entry "Cars You Drive," therapists note that a car can symbolize a relationship. For example, if a husband and wife are in a car together, the dream might be about their relationship, and the answer to the question "Who was driving this car?" often suggests who is in control of this relationship. How the dreamer/passenger feels about the driver often suggests how he or she feels about the other person being in control. I have noted again and again that when a person dreams of someone else driving the car, usually things go very badly in the dream. This suggests that the driver of the car represents either someone in the dreamer's life or an unrecognized aspect of the dreamer's personality that is driving and in control of the dreamer's life.

SAMPLE DREAMS

The Stolen Car

John had a recurring dream that his car was stolen.

When John awoke he realized immediately that the stolen car symbolized his feelings about the woman he had been dating, who was a very controlling person and who had stolen his mobility and his freedom to run his own life. He felt that his engine had been stolen. He broke up with her and stopped having this dream.

My Driving Wife

Wilson dreamt that he and his wife headed somewhere in her car and that he was driving. On their return trip his wife drove, and the whole way back Wilson kept trying to figure out how to get back in the driver's seat.

Wilson described the car as an MG Midget, a cute, fun car, one he liked driving. He felt very uncomfortable when he wasn't driving the car, but the main feeling in the dream was his concern about how he was going to get back in the driver's seat. When I asked him if that reminded him of anything going on in his life right now he responded, "Well, my wife and I are in therapy and we are considering a divorce. I don't want to break up the marriage, but she wants to leave, and I do feel that I'm no longer in control of the situation. Maybe I'm not in control of her anymore. She is also very little."

Squatters Move In

Cassandra dreamt that squatters had moved into her house and that she was unable to move them out. They felt entitled and didn't do much to help take care of the house; they used up the resources in her house; and, insult of insults, they took off with her favorite red car. She was furious and threatened to report the car to the police as stolen.

When Cassandra interviewed herself about the dream, she described squatters as people who take over a property without buying it or paying their dues and who feel entitled to take control of a place that is not theirs. This reminded her of her current boyfriend, who had asked to live in her house for just a couple of weeks but several months later still was not sharing her household expenses although unwilling to move. She had felt sorry for him and had wanted to support him through a difficult period in his life. But the fact that in the dream the squatters had taken off with her car and felt so entitled to the privileges of the household made her recognize how very angry she was at being taken advantage of while her boyfriend played on her sympathies. The car symbolized her private personal energies that no one else had any right to run off with. But that was exactly what her boyfriend was doing, both in the emotional relationship and in the physical living situation.

Unsafe at Any Speed

Julianna dreamt of seeing a car her sister had once owned suddenly appear before her. The car had no driver; it was a Prinz produced by the Germans in the late 1950s. The Prinz was one of the first very tiny cars manufactured, a novelty on the American market at the time. Julianna described it as a fun car that people would play with. In her high school days boys would pick the car up and turn it around on a one-way street. As she continued to describe the car, she said that although it was a whimsical and unusual fun car, she never wanted to own one, because it could never protect her. It was too small, it had no crash protection, and, yes, the name of the car was a Prinz, German for "Prince." This was the nickname of her boyfriend, who, as the bridge became clear, was a man adventurous with finances to the point of often being without any. While she found her boyfriend, like the car, to be exotic, playful, and novel, she knew she could never feel safe in that relationship, either on a financial or an emotional level.

WHAT DO YOU SAY?

See the questions in "Cars You Drive." In addition, you might consider these questions:

1. Describe the person who is driving your car.
2. Describe how well/poorly he or she is driving your car.

3. Do things go well or badly in the dream when the person is at the wheel?

4. How do you feel about the fact that this person is driving?

5. Does this person, whom you describe as (restate the description) and who is driving your car in this way, remind you of any part of yourself or anyone in your life, present or past, who is directing or controlling an important part of your life?

Being Unable to Run

VARIATIONS

Almost everyone in an audience will groan when I mention the dream of wanting to run but being unable to; your legs feel like they are mud or water and you just can't run! This dream is sometimes a variation on the dream of being chased because often people recognize they are unable to run as a result of trying to flee from a pursuer. This dream is usually both frustrating and frightening.

WHAT OTHERS HAVE SAID

Psychoanalysts for years have interpreted the dream of being unable to run as an expression of the dreamer's desire *not* to escape. The dreamer can't run because fundamentally he or she doesn't want to run from the pursuer, who is interpreted as a desired sexual partner. More contemporary interpreters often look for a metaphor in the very fact that the dreamer feels paralyzed, unable to take meaningful action to escape, and they suggest the dreamer may feel stuck and paralyzed in his or her life. Unfortunately, such an interpretation can be exceedingly vague. I have often wondered if this dream is not a regular chase dream from which the dreamer partially wakes but does not gain physical control of the extremities, since the stimulus to our big motor muscles is turned off while we dream. Perhaps we can't move our legs because the body hasn't awakened quite as quickly as the mind. You might want to look up "Being Chased" dreams at the beginning of this section and use those questions and ideas to help you interpret your dream of being unable to run.

SAMPLE DREAM

Leaden Legs

Patrick dreamt: "I was playing softball with a community team and hit the ball into left field and went to run to first base. But my legs wouldn't go, they felt heavy and leaden, and I was unable to get to first base before I woke up."

In interviewing himself, Patrick described his feeling of satisfaction and achievement after hitting the ball, followed by a terrible feeling of not being able to move his legs because they felt so heavy. He felt he was working against tremendous forces. He asked himself where he had similar feelings in waking life and realized that this was a recurring situation in which, having achieved something in his life, he would often feel somewhat paralyzed and unable to follow through. In his work he would win a contract and then have a difficult time motivating himself to do the follow-up. He had always thought this was just laziness, but the feelings in the dream had more to do with anxiety. Perhaps some of his paralysis after achievement came from a fear that the achievement was just a fluke and that he wouldn't be able to live up to his promise.

WHAT DO YOU SAY?

1. Why are you running in this dream?
2. If you are being chased, can you describe who or what is running after you?
3. Describe as specifically as you can, using three or four adjectives, how you felt at being unable to run in the dream.
4. Is there anything or anyone in your life that is like the pursuers in your dream?
5. Is there anywhere in your life where you feel just as you do in the dream (for example, paralyzed, leaden, frozen)?
6. If you find a parallel situation, can you imagine a way to mobilize yourself to take appropriate action, to liberate yourself from a fear or from someone else's control?

Being Unable to Call for Help

VARIATIONS

The dream of being unable to call for help can be a very serious one that many people ignore. In this dream the dreamer is often in a difficult, dangerous, sometimes desperate situation. At the very end the dreamer tries unsuccessfully to call for help or hears someone else in the dream saying the dreamer had better get help. The dreamer calls out but can't make his or her voice heard. Sometimes the dreamer frantically dials 911 or tries to get the operator but can't get through; either the telephone doesn't work or the operator is uncooperative or the dreamer dials the wrong emergency number. In other variations the dreamer goes for help to a trusted friend who is unresponsive or calls out to a trusted friend who never arrives or is not home.

WHAT OTHERS HAVE SAID

At the dream center, Dr. Flowers and I have been amazed at how frequently the dream of calling for help turns out to have its parallel situation in the dreamer's waking life. By asking the dreamer to describe the situation and feelings in the dream and then to see if those feelings mirror waking experience, we usually find that the dreamer is in a difficult emotional or career situation and is unable or unwilling to call for help. In fact, the dreamer may even be quite unaware of the need for help. Usually the help that is needed is help that comes from outside, from someone who is more experienced in the field or who has more psychological expertise.

SAMPLE DREAMS

Lost in the Forest

Sylvana dreamt: "I was in the middle of a forest. I was lost, alone, and very frightened. I just kept calling out for help, but there was no one there to hear me."

In describing her feelings, Sylvana recognized fairly quickly how the dream pictured the general state of her emotional life during the past year. She had just divorced and now felt that her entire life had become a new and somewhat alien and threatening experience. She felt that her friends were not sensitive to her needs, and yet she had been quite shy in asking them for support. She thought she had asked for help, but as we discussed the matter she felt she had not been effective in telling her friends the kind of support she needed. Nor had she sought out support groups or therapy, which she now felt could be useful to her in helping her adjust to a new life.

Man Grabs Me

Wendy had this recurring dream: "I am in a barn, and there is a man who is grabbing me and he wants to hurt me somehow. I cry out for help, I scream, but nothing comes out of my mouth so no one can hear me."

The feelings of being powerless and of not being heard, knowing that she couldn't get any sound out of her voice, reminded Wendy of her early sexual abuse in which her father had threatened her saying that if she told anyone he would kill her. As an adult this dream would recur at times in her life when she felt powerless, trapped, or seriously threatened.

WHAT DO YOU SAY?

1. Describe the painful or dangerous situation in your dream in which you need help.

2. If there is an aggressor, describe him or her (mean, angry, crazy, obsessed, and so forth). Use at least three adjectives, and, if you can, include his or her intent.

3. Is there a circumstance in your current life that is metaphorically similar to the one in the dream?

4. Have you been unable to admit that you need help and unable or unwilling to ask for help from friends or from a professional?

5. Could this dream be a warning that your problem is more severe than you have realized and that you really do need some help to work it out?

Making Love with an Unexpected Partner

VARIATIONS

Have you been surprised in your dreams to find yourself making love with the most unexpected people? These dreams can be nightmares or sweet romances depending, of course, on the identity of your lover and on how you feel about that person. You might make love to your mother or your father, your sister or your brother; you might have sex with someone of the same sex if you are heterosexual or someone of a different sex even though you are gay or lesbian. You might find yourself in bed with someone you had a crush on in childhood, someone from second grade or from high school or from college. Often people find themselves making love to an old boyfriend or girlfriend or to a former husband or wife. This can be a rather shocking experience, or it can be a semisweet one of sadness and longing.

WHAT OTHERS HAVE SAID

Traditional psychoanalysts have often interpreted dreams of making love with unexpected partners as disguised expressions of the dreamer's repressed desire to have sex with forbidden partners: with a parent of the opposite sex or, in the case of a heterosexual dreaming of making love to a same-sex partner, with a gay or lesbian lover. Jungians are more likely to interpret a man's dream of having a lovely sexual encounter with a mysterious and attractive woman as an encounter with his anima or the female part of his soul. The woman making love with a man is seen as gaining more intimate knowledge of her masculine self or the male part of her soul, her animus. Gestalt theorists claim that whoever your dream lover is, that person really represents a certain part of yourself or certain characteristics that you are encountering, either pleasantly or unpleasantly.

Before you come to any conclusions, I would encourage you first to describe the personality of the dream lover as well as the quality of the dream encounter. See if there are any parallels in waking life. The dream lover could indeed represent a part of you, a part of your personality. When you are making love to an absolutely marvelous, wonderful person of the same or different sex, the dream lover could represent an idealized self-image or a situation in which you feel honored and flattered that such a lover would be interested in you. Such dreams come at a time when you are moving to a new level of self-confidence and competence either in relationships or in career or in general self-image and self-esteem. In cases where a heterosexual person dreams of being with someone of the same sex, the key to interpretation, as in the other dreams, is to describe the personality of the dream lover. Usually the dreamer will find that this dream lover is a person whom the dreamer admires and would like to emulate, who is often a bit more accomplished than the dreamer.

Now of course these dreams can also mean the obvious, that the dreamer really does have strong heterosexual, homosexual, or lesbian leanings. However, I have found that this is not often the case. Lesbians and gay men who dream heterosexual dreams are usually just as uncomfortable as are heterosexuals who dream homosexual dreams. Most often these dream lovers represent aspects of the dreamer's current or hoped-for personality and development.

SAMPLE DREAMS

In Bed with My Ex

Larry was surprised to have the following dream: "There I was, having sex with my exwife. I couldn't believe it. I woke up and said, 'What am I doing here?'"

When we asked Larry to describe his ex, he said she was an extremely controlling, critical, and talkative woman whom he had married when he was too young to know any better. We asked why he had married her. He admitted that it was because she was the sexiest, most desirable woman in his college class but that he had failed to notice some of her more enduring and obnoxious personality traits. In order to find out why Larry would have had this dream on this particular night, we asked him if there was anyone in his life now whom he would describe as originally attractive and highly desirable but also critical, controlling, and talkative. Larry said that he was dating one of the prettiest women in the city and that two of his friends had commented that she was somewhat like his first wife. It was very hard for Larry to consider that he might be in bed with the same woman, only this time with a different name and a different face.

Dreams of being in bed with former lovers usually point out a pattern that we are repeating while we pick different people in different bodies. There is a strong tendency to pick similar personalities over and over again until we resolve the needs or conflicts that led us to get involved with that sort of person in the first place. We often ask the dreamer, "When was the very first time you were involved with a person who has the basic personality style of the lover in your dream?" The answer is often a shocked, "Oh, my heavens, it was my mother" or "my father" or "my older brother or sister," some early person in the dreamer's life whom the dreamer seems compelled to connect with again and again.

Sex with a Grammar School Buddy

Katie dreamt that she was having rather boring sex with a boy she hadn't seen since she was in fourth grade. His name was Martin. She woke up asking herself why she would do that. When she interviewed herself about her dream, Katie described Martin as a fun-loving, friendly buddy she'd had at school, not somebody she particularly had a crush on but someone who was almost a brother. When she described the quality of the lovemaking, she said it was very nice, somewhat satisfying, but certainly not erotic or exciting or thrilling or even particularly romantic. Then she asked herself, "Is there any situation in my life in which I feel like this, as if I were with someone who is like Martin, friendly and nice but not particularly erotic or exciting?" She immediately realized that this was a perfect description of her relationship with her husband. It had become a friendly, buddy relationship that left her longing for romance, excitement, and a more erotic experience.

WHAT DO YOU SAY?

1. What is the personality of your dream lover like? If you don't know your lover, describe what he or she seems to be like in the dream.

2. Does your dream lover, whom you describe as (restate the description), remind you of anyone in your current life?

3. If so, does your dream lover highlight important positive or negative aspects of a current relationship?

4. Describe the quality, the feeling, and the flavor of the lovemaking in your dream.

5. Does this remind you of the dynamics of a current or past relationship?

6. How so?

7. Once you find the bridge to a current relationship, see if this is an example of a recurring pattern in your life.

Having Sex with a Famous Person

VARIATIONS

Have you ever dreamt of making love to Bill Clinton, Sean Connery, Denzel Washington, Brad Pitt, Pierce Brosnan, Samuel Ramey, or Andre Agassi? How about Christie Brinkley or Claudia Schiffer, Rita Hayworth, Marilyn Monroe, Vanessa Williams, Sharon Stone? Or have you dreamt of making love to your favorite writer or poet or musician? In your dream you may not actually be making love but may be in an extremely romantic and satisfying situation with your famous dream lover. What happens? Do things go well, or does a crowd of strangers suddenly enter the room just as things are getting really steamy? Or does your famous lover look wonderful and approach you but then disappear or suddenly become too busy to be available to you? Often there is some element of surprise in dreams of sex with famous people.

WHAT OTHERS HAVE SAID

As you might expect, traditional psychoanalysts have often interpreted a famous dream lover according to how he or she fits into the psychoanalytic framework: an older man is likely to be interpreted as a female dreamer's father, and so on. Jungians usually consider a positively viewed famous lover as a guide into the dreamer's inner life, as a representation either of his feminine or her masculine side. Since I find labeling parts of personalities as masculine or feminine to be more limiting than fruitful, in a dream interview I simply ask dreamers to describe the dream lover. Then I ask them if the lover reminds them of anyone in their current life or of any part of themselves or of any force or direction in their lives. I let the dreamers decide whether the dream lover is a self-representation or a representation of someone or some goal in their lives. It is also crucial to describe the quality of lovemaking and the feeling that exists between the lovers in order to find what metaphorical meaning this can carry.

SAMPLE DREAMS

When Bill Clinton was first elected, I received many telephone calls from journalists all over the world asking about Americans who dreamt about making love to the new president. Indeed, I had heard quite a few of these dreams, but, as you would expect, they meant different things to different people. It all depended on how the dreamer felt about Bill and how the action unfolded in the dream.

Clinton on the Run

Stephanie dreamt that she was in a hotel bedroom with Bill Clinton. She was so excited! She admired him, she thought he was extremely handsome, and she loved his power. He was smiling and offering her a glass of wine. Just as they started to kiss he looked at his watch and said, "Sorry, I have to go. I have a meeting." She woke up frustrated.

When Stephanie interviewed herself, she described Bill Clinton as a man of her generation, good-looking, powerful, fun, well-intentioned. She would just love to have sex with him. She felt flattered in the dream that he was interested in her. The only problem was that he was too busy and walked out, leaving her high and dry. When she asked herself if there was anyone in her life she thought of as handsome, as of her own generation, and as powerful and erotic but who was finally too busy to give her what she really wanted, she realized that this was an exaggerated but apt picture of her husband. She admired him and found him very sexy and quite powerful, but he was so busy earning money and prestige that they never had time for truly intimate, erotic encounters. By the way, her husband was president of his own company.

Loving Liz Taylor

Alan dreamt that he was at a beautiful tropical resort in a bungalow making love to none other than Liz Taylor. She was beautiful, bejeweled, and sexy. He said, "I couldn't believe my good fortune in having her in my arms." Describing Liz as if he were describing her to someone who had never heard of her before, Alan said that she was an actress, extremely sexy, that in the dream she was younger than she is now, perhaps in her forties, and that he found her to be a thrilling and somewhat dangerous woman. He knew that she had a history of having many husbands and of having almost any man she wanted. She was reputed to be the most beautiful woman in the world in her younger days. Asked if this description reminded him of anybody in his life, he said that he had just started dating a woman who was somewhat intimidating to him because she was both beautiful and exotic, but that he thought it was worth the risk. In the dream Alan had felt suddenly that it was worth any risk to have this woman in his arms. The dream seemed both a warning and an encouragement. He was entering this relationship with his eyes open.

WHAT DO YOU SAY?

1. Describe your famous dream lover as if you were describing him or her to someone from another planet who has never heard of this person before. Since you probably don't know this famous lover personally, simply describe him or her as well as you can from what you've heard and what you think to be true. Put into words your impression of this dream lover, what you think he or she is like. Use three or four adjectives.

2. Does this dream lover, whom you describe as (restate the description), remind you of anything or anyone in your life or of any part of yourself? If so, how?

3. Describe the situation in the dream and the quality of the lovemaking or the romance.

4. Does this description remind you of any situation in your life?

5. How do you feel in this dream?

6. Is there anywhere in your life where you feel or long to feel as you do in the dream? For example, do you wish that you could be loved by such a person, that you were worthy of such a love? Or do you find, upon awakening, that the sweet romance you had in your dream is something sadly lacking in your current life?

7. How so? Elaborate.

Having Sex with a Co-worker or Friend

VARIATIONS

To dream of making love to someone you work with can be a shocking experience that leaves you feeling awkward and embarrassed when you encounter that person the next day at work. These dreams come in two broad categories. Either you are making love to someone you find very attractive and the dream feels much like a wish-fulfillment dream, or you are making love to someone to whom you are not particularly or in the least bit attracted and you wonder why in the world you would dream such a thing.

As always, the interpretation of this dream depends on the details of the actions and the feelings taking place in it. The lovemaking may be very erotic and everything goes just fine. Or it may be going just fine when suddenly you are interrupted; people enter the room or your partner abruptly gets up and leaves, or, even more shocking, your partner suddenly turns into someone else. Then there are the dreams in which lovemaking is rather tedious or awkward or feels somewhat obligatory.

WHAT OTHERS HAVE SAID

Jungians often look at dreams of intercourse as expressing a need or a desire to come together with, to get closer to, or to embrace the qualities represented by the lover in the dream. These qualities may be qualities within the dreamer or qualities the dreamer has yet to develop. Or they might be destructive characteristics depending, of course, upon the nature of the dream lover.

Anne Faraday, a pioneer in non-dogmatic dream interpretation, writes, "If your dream shows you sexually involved with someone who is not part of your present life, it must be using sex as a metaphor. . . ."[2] At the dream center, we often see sex used as a metaphor for feelings of intimacy, acceptance, rejection, domination, and so forth. But almost as often it seems true that the person you are involved with in the dream represents either a part of yourself or a caricature of someone you are currently involved with. The dream of having sex with Gilbert, whom you haven't seen since fifth grade, may lead you to describe Gilbert as having been a particularly greedy, selfish, insensitive child, and that description may help you see more clearly those traits in your new boyfriend, who has more Gilbert qualities then you cared to recognize. Sex in such a dream can be a metaphor for the quality of intimacy in your relationship, or it could be a comment on the quality of your sexual connection with a man who is like Gilbert in his sexual style.

Faraday also writes, "If your dream shows you being sexually involved with someone in your present toward whom you have no conscious feelings of attraction, then it is almost certainly a straight warning dream."[3] I have found that only rarely are such dreams warning dreams; more frequently, in my experience, the dreamer discovers that the dream lover is usually a caricatured representation of certain traits of the dreamer's current waking lover or a representation, using sex as a metaphor, of a dreamer's other nonsexual relationships either at home or at work. Infrequently, dreamers use such dream lovers to represent parts of themselves. Again, it is important to describe your dream lover and to ask yourself—and no one else—if that person reminds you of someone in your life or some part of yourself.

Our clients at the dream center have come up with many versions of the dream of having sex with a co-worker, and their interpretations are highly varied. If the dream lover is a co-worker to whom the dreamer has felt attracted and if the sex in the dream works well, then we may interpret these dreams to be expressions of wishes that cannot be expressed in the workplace. The dream can then be taken lightly and pleasantly. When an individual dreams of having a sexual encounter with an attractive co-worker but the dream lovemaking is complicated or interrupted, these co-workers may represent someone in the dreamer's personal life. The obstacles in the dream often are active metaphors for the difficulties the dreamer is having in a current, intimate relationship. The interpretation of the dream of making love to an unattractive co-worker, one the dreamer would never consider having sex with, depends entirely upon a good description of the personality and style of the dream lover, the quality of the lovemaking, and the obstacles that appear. Let's look at two of many possible directions such a dream could take.

SAMPLE DREAMS

In Bed with Jack

Mimi was quite surprised by this dream: "I'm in bed making love to Jack Olsen. He's very sexy. I'm really enjoying myself, to my great surprise."

Mimi described Jack as a co-worker who was just a normal sort of guy—pleasant and friendly but not particularly attractive to her. He was also a very reliable, cheerful fellow at work. She said she would never, ever have sex with him. One of the members of our dream study group asked Mimi, "Is there anyone in your life who is like Jack, friendly and reliable, not particularly attractive, sort of a nice, normal sort of guy?" Mimi said no, adding, "I like exotic, unusual men, and I don't know anybody else like him." When asked to describe the quality of the love-making, she said it was rich and warm and sexy. She just couldn't believe it, she felt safe and comfortable with Jack. At this point she started to laugh and said, "You know, I'd like to feel that way with someone. I hardly ever feel really comfortable with my boyfriends or the kinds of men I pick. Still, it's hard to imagine Jack ... maybe someone like Jack. . . ."

Kissing Susie

Jeff, who was the CEO of his firm, had this dream: "I was in my office, and I called in my new assistant, Susie. I kissed her and unbuttoned her blouse, she fondled me, and we started making love. But then just as everything was going wonderfully she slapped me across the face, got up, put on her clothes, and left the office. I was frustrated and puzzled."

In his self-interview Jeff described Susie as a new, young, lovely, sexy, sweet, agreeable assistant who always wanted to please. He described his action in the dream as being somewhat predatory. He knew that he was taking advantage of her, of her subordinate position, and of her desire to keep her job. What seemed out of character was the slap in the face. Jack said he would never really do such a thing, so maybe the dream was a wish. But then why the slap in the face? His imaginary interviewer asked him, "Is there anyone in your life who is like Susie? In other words, who is cute, young, and attractive, who is subordinate to you, and of whom you take advantage? Someone who feels it financially necessary to make sure you are pleased?" Jack thought, "That really reminds me of my wife. She is not as young as Susie, but she is beautiful and is definitely subordinate, feels dependent, and tries to please me a lot. That's interesting. Last night she told me she would no longer come to company dinners with me if I refused to go dancing at least once a week. I guess it's pretty egotistical of me, but that felt like a slap in the face."

WHAT DO YOU SAY?

1. Describe your dream lover (using at least three or four adjectives) as if you were describing the lover to someone who has never heard of or seen him or her before.

2. What is the lover like in your dream?

3. Is there anyone in your life or any part of yourself that is like this lover, whom you describe as (restate the description)?

4. Describe the action or the quality of lovemaking in the dream.

5. How are you feeling in the dream?

6. Are these feelings familiar? When have you felt this way?

7. Is there any situation in your life that is like the one in the dream, which you describe as (restate the description)?

8. How does making love with this particular co-worker describe a situation in your life?

Being Coerced to Have Sex

VARIATIONS

Among the most uncomfortable dreams people have are those of being obliged or somehow coerced to have sex. As you might imagine, women have this dream far more frequently than do men, but for both sexes it is a thoroughly unpleasant, often painful experience. Such a dream may consist of coercion by armed men. Frequently the dreamer is obliged to have sex with a family member. In the mild versions the dreamer is not forced to have sex but must submit to being looked at or being undressed and exposed in a sexual manner. In other scenes the dreamer watches someone else, adult or child, being exposed or watches another person being forced into a sexual encounter. Sometimes the dreamer tries to save the person who is being coerced but is incapable of rescuing the person being abused. Often the dreamer runs to save herself and suffers intense guilt for abandoning the victim. Feelings of shame and anger, fear and helplessness are often paramount in these dreams.

WHAT OTHERS HAVE SAID

Many traditional psychoanalysts interpret sexual coercion in a dream as a disguised wish on the part of the dreamer to have sex either with the person pictured in the dream or with someone else who is interpreted as being represented by the dream figure. Such a therapist, for example, might interpret the dreamer's being forced into a sexual encounter with a neighbor to be a disguised expression of the wish of the female dreamer to have sex with her father. Even the contemporary Jungian therapist Karen Signell writes, "So images of rape in a woman's fantasies or dreams don't need to be interpreted *concretely* as an actual desire to be assaulted sexually, dominated, or degraded, but can usually be interpreted *metaphorically* as a desire for something missing in a woman herself or her partner in their internal dramas of yielding to sexuality."[4]

I have written at length on this extremely important subject in my book *Sensual Dreaming,* and my many years of research have led me to take this issue very seriously. After many interviews with dreamers, I have come to the conclusion that sexual coercion in dreams is almost always an expression of feeling coerced, controlled, threatened, and violated in waking life. These dreams seem to express, not a contrary wish, but rather the pain and anguish of the dreamer who finds herself in a situation analogous to the one pictured in the dream. The dreamer may feel coerced into certain circumstances at work or may feel controlled and threatened within a relationship. The coercion and the threat may not be sexual in nature; however, very often they are.

Signell and many others recognize that dreams of rape or sexual trauma can stem from posttraumatic stress in the dreams of women who have been sexually abused. These dreams express the feelings of terror, vulnerability, guilt, and shame that such experiences leave with the victim. I am sad to say that many dreams of sexual coercion are red flags for undiscovered or unremembered sexual abuse in early childhood. This fact is missed by many who are too quick to interpret the sexual coercion as a metaphor or disguise for the wish of sexual release. It is true that in waking life, fantasies of being coerced sexually often serve to release the fantasizer from feelings of guilt or shame and to allow him or her to accept pleasure with less conflict, since, after all, he or she is no longer responsible for all this pleasure. However, in waking fantasies we are in control of the action and we're not frightened by it; we use it for our own purposes, usually to turn ourselves on.

In dreams the situation is entirely different; the sexual coercion feels totally real and in almost all cases feels highly uncomfortable, usually terrifying. The function of sexual coercion in a dream is, in my opinion, vastly different from that in waking fantasies and must be respected as a possible sign of enormous and painful sexual conflict on the part of the dreamer. In a fantasy of coercion or rape we know we are safe; in dreams we do not. In dreams we are almost always totally taken up by the experience, which is very real and very threatening.

If you have recurring dreams of being sexually abused or coerced, you probably also at various times in your life have wondered if you were sexually abused, or you may actually remember such abuse. I encourage you to read chapter 8 of *Sensual Dreaming* and to see a therapist or join a support group. While sexual abuse is a wound that is difficult to heal entirely, you can make your life much better if you are willing to do good therapeutic work.

Not all dreams of sexual coercion reflect sexual abuse; they do, however, reflect conflict that may or may not be sexual in nature. You may choose to use images of sexual coercion to help you recognize ways you are feeling cornered, held down, or violated at work, within a relationship, or in your family environment. The way the dream ends will say much about how you are coping with the situation. You may find yourself angry and thinking of ways to liberate yourself, or you may be planning revenge, or, in the most desperate case, you may feel totally helpless and terrified, unable to think of or create within a dream any resources to rescue yourself from your situation. These feelings usually parallel the ones you feel in waking life and will help you identify the area of concern for your particular dream.

SAMPLE DREAMS

Gun Rape

Regina dreamt: "I was running through the streets of Boston on a rainy night, and a strange, evil man was chasing me. He had a gun, and the next thing I knew we were in an alley. He had torn off my clothing and was holding the gun up my vagina. I woke up screaming."

Regina awoke feeling totally helpless and terrified. When I asked her if she remembered having felt like this before she tearfully admitted that she had when her father had threatened to kill her if she ever told anyone of his sexual abuse. A series of Regina's dreams similar to this one helped her to confront the trauma of her past, which she had preferred to pretend she had forgotten. Over time she realized that her inability to develop a close intimate relationship was due in large part to her generalized fear of men and her inability to trust, since one of the people she had most trusted had betrayed her when she was a little child.

Subway Rapist

Wendy dreamt: "I'm on a subway, and there is a man in the car who is staring at me. He walks over to me and puts his hand on top of my hand. I know that he is going to rape me. I am frozen with fear."

When I interviewed Wendy she told me she had had this dream for three years and did not remember having had any dream like it previous to that time. Asked to describe the man, she said he was dark, determined, handsome, and extraordinarily controlling. I asked her, "What is rape?

Pretend I come from another planet and have never heard of it before." She said, "Oh, it's not a sexual act, it's an act of power and domination. This man wanted to totally dominate me, and I was too afraid to react." I asked her, "Is there anyone in your life who is like this man, who is dark, determined, handsome, and extraordinarily controlling and who basically tells you that he is going to dominate you and to whom you respond with frozen fear?" Her eyes opened wide and she said, "Oh, that's just like my boyfriend whom I've just broken up with. He was my boyfriend for exactly three years, and for the whole time he was extremely dominating, and I, at the age of twenty, was too stupid to protest. I felt that I had to do whatever he told me. He never sexually abused me, but emotionally he did."

WHAT DO YOU SAY?

1. Describe the sexual coercion going on in your dream.

2. Describe the perpetrator in your dream. What is he like? If he is a stranger, describe what he is wearing, what his intent seems to be, and how he is acting.

3. Given a person who wears these clothes, who looks like this, and who acts like this, what would you think such a person would be like? (Use three or four adjectives to describe the personality such a person would have.)

4. Is there anything in your life, any part of yourself, or anyone in your life who is like this person whom you describe as (restate the description)?

5. Does the action in your dream, which you describe as (restate the description), remind you of any situation in your life?

6. Do your feelings in your dreams, which you describe as (restate the description of feelings), remind you of similar feelings you have in your life? If so, where and when?

7. Does the way you cope with or respond to the coercion in your dream help you to see more clearly a similar situation in your life to which you have a habit of responding in the way you do in the dream?

Once you have identified the area of your life your dream is commenting on, ask yourself if there is anything you can do on your own to change the situation or if getting help and support from friends or professionals would give you the boost that you need to reduce the discomfort or the anguish.

Having Sex with a Former Lover

VARIATIONS

Having sex with a former lover or spouse in a dream can be a touching and joyous or excruciating and shocking experience. It all depends upon whether you like and enjoy the lover in your dream and upon how the actual lovemaking unfolds. You may find yourself with the best lover you ever had, someone you haven't seen for years and for whom you still hold a special place in your heart. You may wake up from the dream sad to realize that you don't have a partner who makes you feel as special as he did, and you may long for the special, loving, tender, or erotic qualities that you haven't had in a relationship since you knew that lover. On the other hand, you may dream of being in bed with a former lover who was difficult, critical, and withholding. Or perhaps your returned dream lover was inept sexually or was a sexual plunderer who used you and discarded you. From these dreams you probably wake up relieved and puzzled as to why you would put yourself through all that yet one more time.

WHAT OTHERS HAVE SAID

Old-fashioned psychoanalysts and others who presume that dream images try to disguise the real identity of the person the dreamer is concerned with have interpreted these dreams as disguised wishes on the part of the dreamer to have sex with the analyst or the dreamer's parent. Jungians sometimes interpret these dreams as describing the dreamer's relationship to his or her contrasexual masculine or feminine side. I have found such theorizing unnecessary. When I ask dreamers to describe their dream lovers and then to consider if these descriptions remind them of anyone or any part of themselves, the dreamers are usually quite capable of identifying the dream image as representing some aspect of themselves or, as is often the case, as representing a repetitive pattern in the dreamers' romantic and/or sexual lives. Two such examples follow.

SAMPLE DREAMS

Left Out in the Cold

Lola dreamt that she was in bed with her first husband. As usual, he was very turned on by her and delighted to have intercourse with her. She, however, felt like no more than a vessel to provide and receive his pleasure. He was entirely uninterested in an intimate exchange of pleasure and of feeling. She woke up with a start.

Asked to describe her dream lover, Lola said the exhusband in her dream was exactly like her real exhusband, who indeed was a very selfish, if enthusiastic, lover with whom she did not enjoy having sexual relations. Asked how the lovemaking went in the dream, she said it was typical. "He was intensely attracted to me; that's flattering. But

he leaves me out in the cold, he's just there for his own pleasure." I asked her if there was anyone in her life currently
who acted the way her exhusband did in the dream. She
said, "Not really. Well, perhaps a little bit. My current
boyfriend is a little bit like that. In fact, maybe he's a lot like
that. But I keep hoping that he'll change." Upon hearing
her words, Lola laughed, knowing that thinking your partner will change is a dangerous myth. I asked Lola if, in her
history of relationships with men, there were ever any other
men who treated her like this—men who were very attracted to her, very enthusiastic about sex, but who left her
in the cold and weren't interested in an intimate exchange
of feelings. She responded that being a beautiful, tall, blue-
eyed blond, she seems to have attracted, and accepted, a lot
of these men. In fact, to her dismay, she realized that her father had been very much that way with her mother. She saw
then that her dream was showing her a pattern in her love
life and forcing her to see how much her current boyfriend,
while he might have a different body and different name,
was just a repeat of the same sort of guy.

Smile on My Face

Cory dreamt: "I was making passionate and yet very tender love with a man who was like two of my previous
lovers. He was warm like Michael but energetic and competent like Frederick. It was wonderful, just wonderful. I
woke up with a smile on my face."

Asked to describe Michael, Cory said that he was a
warm, tender, gentle man but that he could hardly earn a
living and was rather passive. It was hard for her to stay
with him because he was rather timid and boring, but she
loved his gentleness. She described Frederick as a business

tycoon who was afraid of no challenge, who was exciting, passionate, and well cultured but a little rough around the edges. He didn't have much time for romance because he was always busy slaying corporate dragons. She went on to say this dream was a perfect picture of being with the perfect man who had both tenderness and dynamism. "This could be just a wish-fulfillment dream, but I still have hope. I won't be happy with either one or the other. I have to have both qualities in a man."

WHAT DO YOU SAY?

1. Describe your dream lover. What is his or her personality like, and how did you feel with this person in waking life?

2. How does the lovemaking go in the dream?

3. Is there anyone in your life who is like this lover whom you describe as (restate the description) and with whom you feel the way you felt in the dream? (You may find it hard to admit it if this is an unpleasant dream and the dream lover reminds you of a current lover for whom you still have high hopes. Be patient with yourself, and seek out your most honest feelings.)

4. Have there been any other lovers in your life who repeat the pattern you see in your dream?

5. When was the very first time you had any relationship with a person who was like the lover in your dream?

6. If this dream has helped you to identify repetitive patterns in your romantic relationships, what might you do to change them if you do not find them satisfying?

Having Sex with Family Members

VARIATIONS

The shocking dream of sex with a family member usually comes as a big surprise to the dreamer. You may be having sex with a boyfriend who suddenly turns into your father! You may be having pleasant, comfortable sex with a brother or a sister, an aunt or an uncle and wake up worrying that you have incestuous desires. On the other hand, you may have dreams of being sexually coerced by family members, in which case you might want to look at the entry "Being Coerced to Have Sex." Finding yourself in a sexual encounter with a family member in a dream can go from being mildly uncomfortable to being shocking to being brutally violent. Other dreams can actually be pleasant, although this is much less common. Not infrequently the female dreamer who is being forced into sex with an older family member calls out for help in the dream, but no one answers. Many people who have such dreams feel great shame because they do not understand that at some point or another almost everyone dreams of having sex with a parent. If these dreams are frequent and upsetting, they can suggest early sexual abuse. If this has happened to you, to a friend, or to one of your children, remember that the child is never the responsible or guilty party. The adult is.

WHAT OTHERS HAVE SAID

In 200 C.E. Artemidorus gave many interpretations for dreams of interfamilial sex. He interpreted sexual intercourse that was natural and legal differently than he did intercourse that was illegal and unnatural. Artemidorus believed that important dreams foretold future events and that sexual dreams were no exception.

While his predictive interpretations may seem simplistic, it is interesting to note his appreciation for the power of metaphors. For example, he wrote, "To possess a son who is not yet five years old signifies, I have observed, the child's death. That the dream should have this meaning is quite understandable, since a small child will be corrupted and we call corruption death. If the child is more than five years old but less than ten, he will be sick and the dreamer will be involved in some disgrace as a result of some thoughtless undertaking. The child, because he has been possessed while he is still too young, will suffer pain and, in this way, will be sick. The dreamer will be disgraced because of his foolishness. For no man with any self-control at all would possess either his own son or any other child of so tender an age. . . ." He went on, "But if a man dreams that he has sexual intercourse with a married daughter, she will leave her husband and come to him so that she is with him and lives with him."[5]

Traditionally, psychoanalysts have held that such dreams suggest the internal censor was ineffective in disguising the deep, unconscious Oedipal wishes of the dreamer. Some modern psychoanalysts now depart from this traditional position. They recognize that at least some of these dreams might not reflect a wish for intercourse with the family member but rather might express the dreamer's wish to break through superego inhibitions using the shocking content to rally conscious support against uncontrolled infantile drives for incestuous gratification.[6]

Incestuous dreams have been dealt with by most major dream theorists, almost all of whom recognize that such a dream can express a wish, a memory of actual incest, or a fear. It may also represent a metaphorical description of the dreamer's feeling about an actual family member who plays the role of the lover in the dream. Ancient Greeks and certain Jungians see in a man's dreams of making love to his mother a return to a motherland or a regression to childhood and protection by the mother as well as the possibility that such a dream represents the dreamer's reconnection with the feminine mother principle or archetype.

As usual, it is impossible to interpret a dream accurately without looking at the context of the action of the dream. In this case it is necessary to understand both how the love-making is going and what the dreamer's and dream lover's feelings are. Once elicited from the dreamer, this material can then be used to seek out parallels in the dreamer's waking life.

SAMPLE DREAMS

José Turns into Father

Trisha dreamt: "I was making love to my boyfriend, José. He was very romantic and very forceful. He became more and more dominant. I opened my eyes, and he had turned into my father! I woke up with a start."

In our interview I asked Trisha to describe José. What was his personality, what was his lovemaking style? She described José as a warm, tender Latin, but also as a slightly too macho male. "I love his passion, but he overdoes it at times." When I asked her if this reminded her of anyone else in her life she said, "No, that really is a good picture of my feelings toward, and my relationship with, José."

I asked her to describe how the lovemaking went, and she said it became more and more domineering and she didn't like it. I asked her if in any way her relationship with

José was moving along these lines, either sexually or emotionally. She said she was afraid it might, but so far it was tolerable. When I asked her to describe her father, she said, "He is a very dominant man, not very good at knowing what he's feeling. That's very different from José. Dad has to control everything, and I hate that." I asked, "How did you like being in bed with your father or someone like your father?" She replied, "It was horrible. I would have a terrible life with him, he is just too controlling." I asked her, "Is there any way you see José, who is warm and emotional but tends to be too domineering and macho at times, turning into your father, who is extremely domineering and controlling of everything?" Trisha said, "I think in my dreams I have more worries about José being like my father than I'm willing to admit in my waking life." Trisha's dream was not about wanting to have sex with her father. It was a typical dream helping Trisha to look more closely at the emotional similarity between her boyfriend and her father—a similarity that, left unrecognized, could cause her a great deal of trouble in the future.

Sex with My Brother

Louisa dreamt: "I was sleeping in my childhood bedroom at home. My husband, Joe, snuck into my room and started to fondle me. But somehow I knew it was really my brother. I was afraid to call out because I knew he would hurt me if I told anyone."

In our interview Louisa described her brother as a bully who in fact sexually abused her for approximately three years during her adolescence. He would come into the bedroom and have sex play with her and a few times had intercourse. She was very afraid of him and never told anyone. She knew about her sexual abuse and had undergone psychotherapy to resolve some of her pain. However, this dream recurred at the age of thirty when she was married to her husband, Matt. When I asked her to describe Matt, she said, "Well, he is furtive and sneaky; he doesn't want anyone to know the details of his life. In the dream he was very much like my brother; he was a bully, a pushy bully." I asked her if there was anyone in her life right now who was acting like a pushy bully. She said, "Well, actually, if I'm brutally honest, my husband is. He doesn't sexually abuse me as my brother did, but he sort of corners me, co-erces me, and I have some of that same feeling. More im-portantly, I respond to him very often the way I responded to my brother. I do what he tells me, and I let him intimi-date me. As I talk about this now I am very angry that I'm letting him treat me the way that I let my older brother treat me."

Sex here is a metaphor for domination, coercion, and just plain bullying. If you have had many troubling dreams and sexual dreams, let me suggest that you read my book *Sensual Dreaming,* especially chapter 8, and then talk to a therapist about these dreams so that you can free yourself from some of the discomfort they indicate.

WHAT DO YOU SAY?

1. Describe your dream lover. Who is he or she? What is this person like?
2. Is there anyone in your life, in the present or the past, who is like the person you are having sex with in the dream?
3. Describe the lovemaking in your dream.
4. How do you feel during the dream sex?
5. Are these feelings familiar?
6. If so, in what situation do you feel the way you feel in the dream?

7. Do the situation and feelings you describe while you are with someone who is like (restate the description of the person) remind you of any current situation in your life?

8. If so, how?

9. If the dream action reminds you only of your past circumstances, ask yourself why you might be dreaming this dream at this particular time in your life. Has there been some recent event or relationship in your life that could trigger the memory of such feelings?

Your Love Runs Off with Someone Else

VARIATIONS

Hurt, jealousy, rage—these are the wrenching feelings dreamers report when they dream of their lover running off with another person. In the dream you may know exactly who your lover is leaving you for, or you may have only a general description—a sexy blond or a wealthy hunk. If you are like most of my clients and friends, you wake up feeling terrible and insecure, and you can't wait to tell your lover what you dreamt. You may be worried that your dream is telling you about a hidden love affair. You know that your dream is telling you about insecurity, and you probably are about to give your lover the third degree.

WHAT OTHERS HAVE SAID

In my private office I have seen everyone's worst fears come true. That is, sometimes the dreamer has used the dream to make herself face the fact that her lover really is having an affair with someone else. She may have suspected this but did not want to admit it. In the dream perhaps she put two and two together in a way she could no longer deny. However, the good news is that frequently this dream has nothing to do with an actual affair; rather, the dream deals with issues in the relationship. The dream mistress is often a representation of aspects of the dreamer herself. At other times the dream mistress is a personification of the dreamer's insecurities and fears. A person who is too dependent upon her lover for her sense of self-esteem will be overly jealous and suspicious and is likely to have dreams like this regularly. Hopefully, they will trigger her discussing them with her partner and perhaps with a therapist in order to develop a more secure and satisfying relationship for both partners.

A man may dream of his new girlfriend often leaving him for other men. This may be a very insecure man, but it may also be a dreamer who while unconscious realizes his girlfriend is not ready to commit to him. In waking life he is overconfident; in his dreams he faces his fears.

SAMPLE DREAMS

My Husband Leaves Me for a Blond

Pearl had the following dream, which is not an uncommon one for brunettes: "Gilles and I were in my bedroom. He got out of bed, went to the door, and waved good-bye. I knew he was leaving me for a sexy blond, and I cried myself awake."

I asked Pearl to describe her rival. She said, "Well, all I know is that she was a sexy blond." I asked her to pretend I come from another planet and to tell me what sexy blonds are like. She said, "They offer men easy sex. A man looks at a sexy blond, and that's all he can think of. The blond doesn't demand that the man have a relationship with her; she is happy to be his pretty ornament, and he is happy to have an uncomplicated relationship." I asked her if there was anyone in her life or in her boyfriend's life or any part of herself that was like this sexy blond who didn't ask for anything but a simple relationship. Pearl said that was how she was with her boyfriend for the first year of their relationship. Even though she was a brunette, she said, she had pretty much the style of a sexy blond. Now she wanted a deeper, more meaningful relationship with her boyfriend, and she was running into trouble. Her boyfriend would say things like, "Can't we just have a nice, simple relationship like we used to have?" Pearl understood her dream to be saying that her boyfriend was having a lot of trouble making the emotional shift she wanted and that she indeed was afraid she would lose him to another woman who acted the way she had at the beginning of their relationship. She also said she simply was no longer willing to tolerate such superficial interaction and that she had to risk losing her boyfriend in order to develop the kind of relationship she wanted to have in her life with him or with someone else.

Sexy Macho Men

For the first year of his relationship with Pam, Edgar dreamt repeatedly of her going off with a sexy, audacious, very aggressive man on a motorcycle or in a sports car. In each case his heart was broken.

When he described the various dream rivals, he said they were all highly sexual, macho men. He said that he understood that his girlfriend was a highly sexual woman and that he was worried he would not be able to satisfy her. He was haunted by these dreams of her leaving him for another man. He was quite sure of her fidelity in the moment, but he was very insecure about it in the future. He came to understand these dreams as an expression of his chronic insecurity with this woman, an issue they both needed to address.

WHAT DO YOU SAY?

1. Describe your lover in the dream and the feelings between you.
2. Describe the personality and style of your dream rival.
3. Is there anyone in your life, any part of yourself, or anyone in your lover's life who is like this rival whom you describe as (restate the description of this person)? (Take your time and look carefully for a match.)
4. Do you think this dream reflects your insecurities and your fears or your suspicions of an actual affair?
5. Does the dream action describe a theme in your relationship, such as a realization that your lover is not as committed as you are or that you have trouble trusting?
6. How so? (Clarify your perceptions and your feelings to see what conclusions you can draw from them.)

Losing Your Purse or Wallet

VARIATIONS

You may be anywhere at any time in your dreams, and suddenly notice you've lost your purse, your wallet, or your briefcase. You might feel mildly concerned, but more likely you feel panicky and are unable to remember where your purse is or when or how you lost it.

WHAT OTHERS HAVE SAID

You will probably not be surprised to know that orthodox psychoanalysts interpreted purses as wombs and that losing one's purse could mean losing one's virginity or femininity. Many Jungians interpret such dreams as a loss of identity and often of power, since what we usually keep in our purses and wallets are our identification papers, our credit cards, and our money. Most of our students at the dream center, when asked to describe a purse or a wallet, will say as much, and usually such dreams help them take a closer look at feelings of disorientation, loss of identity or purpose in life, and loss of power. These dreams seem to come most frequently to people who have just retired or who have stepped into a new phase of life, for instance, mothers whose children have grown up and left home. These people often feel unclear about what to do next and about their role in life. Who are they, and how are they going to have currency in their social world now that their former roles have ended?

SAMPLE DREAMS

Lost Purse

Marjorie dreamt: "I was walking downtown, and I suddenly noticed that I had lost my purse. I don't know if it had been stolen by a pickpocket or if I had dropped it, but I realized I had no money left with me at all, and I started looking everywhere. I realized that I would never find it."

In interviewing Marjorie I said, "Now pretend I come from another planet. Why would a human such as yourself care whether or not she loses a purse?" She said, "Oh my, if I lost my purse I would lose all of my identity papers, my credit cards, my money. I would have trouble getting anywhere, making phone calls, buying anything, or proving who I am." I asked her, "Is there anywhere in your life that you feel that you have trouble proving who you are, that you don't have any money, that you don't have any credit cards?" "Oh, yes!" she said. "I don't work any longer, my children are married, and they have children who are almost grown, and I don't think I count for much anymore. I don't know how to tell people I am an important person. I have thoughts, I have desires, I have plans. People treat me like an old person. Actually, I'm not really sure what my plans are, but I want to have plans. I want to be taken seriously, but I do feel old and maybe I don't even take myself that seriously anymore."

Stolen Wallet

In a somewhat unusual version of the stolen wallet dream, Nicholas dreamt that he was walking in a particularly beautiful plaza in Rome when a very handsome young man rushed up to him, stole his wallet, and then disappeared.

I asked Nicholas, "What are wallets, and why do you feel a need to carry one?" He said, "You carry a wallet to put the money you need for the present, your credit cards, and your identification papers in one place." When asked what would be the problem in losing your wallet, he said, "Well, I could replace everything in it, but it would be a lot of trouble. I'd have to go through a lot of bureaucratic red tape to get all my papers replaced. The cash money wouldn't be a problem and the credit cards wouldn't be a problem, but it would be a big bother." I asked him if there was anything in his life that he felt would be a big bother to replace, that gave him a sense of power in the world, like a wallet, and that allowed him to identify himself. He answered, "It's funny, but my girlfriend—I think of my girlfriend. She is extremely beautiful, and everyone notices whenever I go to a party with her. I think it makes me look good. Actually, last night she was flirting with a handsome younger man, and I was afraid that he would steal her from me. It would be a bother to find someone else who is as pretty as she is and as easy to get along with." It is interesting to note that Nicholas was not panicked in the dream; his focus was on what a bother it would be to replace the materials in his wallet. It seems that for Nicholas, his girlfriend was a replaceable treasure.

WHAT DO YOU SAY?

Keep in mind that your dream of a lost purse or wallet, while having common interpretations that are on the mark for most dreamers, may have an idiosyncratic twist that belongs only to your life and your experience. The only way you will find out what your dream means is to interview yourself. Why not try asking yourself these interview questions?

1. What is a purse (or wallet or briefcase)? Pretend I come from another planet and have no idea what one is, why humans use them, or what they carry in them.
2. Why would a human such as yourself care if your purse were stolen or lost?
3. How do you feel in the dream when your purse is lost or stolen?
4. Is there anywhere in your life where you feel the way you feel in the dream when you realize that your purse has been stolen?
5. How so? Be as specific as you can.
6. Having identified the relevant area of your life, is there anything you could do to change the situation?

Being Lost

VARIATIONS

The dream of being lost can be a long or short one. It can go from a simple image of wandering and of feeling lost in a forest, an urban landscape, or a field to a long and involved whodunit chase scene where you end up lost, disoriented, not knowing how to get home. You may be in a storm or even barefoot and feel totally unprepared for the long trek home. You may call out for help and find none. More often, there will be nobody around from whom you can ask assistance. Dreamers usually feel sad and frightened at the end of such dreams.

WHAT OTHERS HAVE SAID

Most psychotherapists recognize dreams of being lost as fairly transparent expressions of the dreamer's feeling lost in an emotional sense in his or her everyday life. The dreamer may have no sense of direction regarding a career or purpose in life, may feel lost in a spiritual sense, or may feel terribly alone, without the ability to form meaningful interpersonal relationships. It is very important not to ignore such dreams, because they can offer the dreamer a chance to identify a core feeling that colors most of the dreamer's waking experience. Sometimes the dreams carry with them clues as to why the dreamer is lost and thus offer the dreamer a chance to make constructive changes.

SAMPLE DREAMS

Lost on the Beach

Penelope dreamt: "I was walking with my husband on the beach, and the sun was out, when suddenly a tidal wave appeared and broke over us. I was fine, but my husband had disappeared. I didn't know where I was anymore. I didn't know which way was home. I didn't see any landmarks. I knew I was lost, and I was frightened."

In our interview I asked Penelope how it felt to be walking with her husband at the opening of the dream. She said it was wonderful, it was warm, and it gave her a perfect picture of her marriage to her very loving husband. I asked her, "What is a tidal wave? Pretend I come from another planet and have never heard of one before. What is it?" She said, "Oh, it's an overwhelming force that destroys everything in its path." When I asked her, "Is there anything in your life that is an overwhelming force, that destroys everything in its path, and that causes your husband to disappear?" she said, "Well, actually, my husband has cancer. He is dying, and it feels like a tidal wave. We've been married for thirty years, and I'm afraid I will be very lost without my husband. This dream seems to be preparing me, actually warning me to prepare myself for the inevitable."

Are My In-Laws Aliens?

Julia dreamt: "It's a rainy, cold night, and I'm in a city. It is very late, I'm all alone, and there is no one around. I know if I stay out in the streets very long I will be in great danger of being attacked by street people, but I feel lost and I don't know how to get out of the part of town I'm in. I don't trust anybody where I am, and I just don't know how to get out. I feel lost and very pressured to hurry and figure it out, because I am in great danger."

Julia described the urban environment she was in as very threatening. People there were of a different race, and she felt they were hostile toward her. She knew she had to get out because she felt she could be attacked at any moment. I asked her if she was in any environment right now where she felt people would be hostile toward her just because she was of a different race. She said that was exactly how she felt when she visited her in-laws. In fact, she said, "That's how I feel whenever I am anywhere near them. They are a very powerful family, and I feel that they are always ready to attack me. But I keep trying to fit in. In the dream all I want to do is get out." I said, "Tell me how it is to feel lost in the dream." She responded, "I feel lost because I don't know how to get out, I don't know where to go, and I feel helpless." I asked her, "Is there anywhere in your life where you feel helpless the same way you do in the dream?" She said, "Oh, yes, I do feel trapped in this in-law environment. They have tried to control my whole life, and I don't know how to get out. I don't want to leave my husband, I just want to get away from them." This dream did not solve Julie's problems, but instead it helped her see how serious they were, how very upset she was, how very attacked she felt, and how lost and incapable she felt of figuring out how to extricate herself from this situation.

WHAT DO YOU SAY?

1. Describe the scene in which you are lost in your dream.
2. How does it feel to be lost? Be as specific as you can.

3. Is there anywhere in your life you have experienced these same feelings—in your family life, your career life, or your spiritual life?

4. How so? Elaborate; be as specific as you can.

5. What do you think you might do to remedy this situation?

Laughing Dreams, Crying Dreams

VARIATIONS

Have you ever awakened giggling and laughing your head off from a dream? Any silly or funny action in a dream can cause you to wake up filled with laughter. What a wonderful way to greet a new day! Then there are the dreams that wet your pillow, dreams from which you awaken feeling very deeply saddened—scenes of reuniting with or losing once again loved ones who have died or dreams of separation from or abandonment by people you love in your waking life. These dreams can lead you to greet the day with tears in your eyes. The intensity of emotions that we are capable of feeling in our dreams is remarkable.

WHAT OTHERS HAVE SAID

Students have told me of dreams of waking in laughter from a fun, lighthearted dream that helped break the spell of a sad mood that may have lasted for weeks. Luckily, some of these dreamers have been able to use the gaiety from the dream to infuse the day with a new levity, which can come as a great respite if the person has been coping with a recent loss or trauma. Crying dreams, on the other hand, usually express a depth of sadness of which the dreamer had been unaware or with which she or he has been unable to cope. Exploring the content of these dreams can help the dreamer confront repressed or inadequately understood feelings in order to work them through and thus alleviate them. If we keep in mind that dreams tell us how we really feel and what we really think, we can use these dreams to help us change our moods and heal our hurts.

My Dog Made Me Laugh

Sylvia dreamt: "I saw my puppy, Suzette, playing with a ball, jumping up and down and acting generally silly. I don't know what it was about the dream, but Suzette just struck me as being so funny! I awoke feeling wonderful."

Sylvia said that this dream came at a very stressful time in her life. She was involved with a lawsuit, her father was ill, and her marriage wasn't going very well. She said the dream didn't comfort her about any of those issues but rather reminded her that in spite of it all she could laugh. It showed her she could remember that playfulness, even in isolated areas, such as playing with her dog, helped her bear the pain and discomfort of this period in her life.

Hugged by an Angel

Harold dreamt that he saw his beloved, deceased wife walk up to him and give him a loving embrace. He broke down, burst into tears, and awoke.

Harold felt that this dream had opened his heart again. He had prematurely terminated his mourning for his wife by sealing off some of the feelings in his heart. While this dream was very sad for him, he understood that the dream served the important function of helping him to face his pain, to bear it, and so to live more fully without numbing himself. Eventually he would feel not only less pain but also more pleasure in life.

WHAT DO YOU SAY?

1. Describe the situation about which you are laughing or crying in the dream. Exaggerate the feelings, amplify them, and describe them.

2. Where in your life, if you are really honest with yourself, would you say you feel the way you feel in the dream?

3. If you were laughing, why do you think you might have a dream of breaking into laughter at this time in your life?

4. Why do you think you had a crying dream at this time? Do you have unfinished grieving or mourning to do? Are you willing to bear the pain of going through this natural process?

5. If you think the crying in your dream is chronic and is the symptom of depression, why not call a psychiatrist and check it out?

Angry Dreams

VARIATIONS

Well, you really told him off, didn't you? Didn't it feel good to get that anger off your chest? We are often very surprised to find ourselves angry in a dream, but dreams may be our first clue that we are repressing feelings of irritation, anger, and hurt. Angry dreams can be very refreshing, and, of course, they can also be very painful. Let's talk about the refreshing ones first.

Dreams provide us a forum for expressing our feelings fully. Sometimes we take advantage of that opportunity by telling our friends, our colleagues, our neighbors, our bosses, our parents, our lovers, or our partners just how angry we are at them and how we are not going to put up with certain behaviors. We let them know how much they have hurt us and how offended we are. It's amazing how eloquently angry we can be in our sleep and how refreshed and relieved we can feel after such a dream.

At times, of course, this expression of anger is tied to a great deal of pain. Women, particularly, both in waking and in sleeping, may find it difficult to be angry without also crying. Of course, both sexes have dreams in which anger is just a first layer, and underneath it lies buried hurt. We can get to that hurt in dreams sometimes by telling someone off, by being very angry, and by saying what we are angry about in the waking state, in an almost directly literal sense. Then we may end the dream by feeling sad because the very thing that made us so angry also hurt our feelings.

WHAT OTHERS HAVE SAID

Most contemporary dream analysts fully appreciate that one of the functions of dreaming is to allow people to feel and express intense emotion. Since anger is a feeling many of us are uncomfortable expressing while awake, dreams can serve a compensatory function of allowing us to get it off our chests. The particular details of the dream will signal the dreamer exactly which area of life he or she is contending with in the dream.

SAMPLE DREAMS

Trashy Neighbor

Caroline dreamt that her very difficult and selfish neighbor had left his trash in her yard. She confronted him, saying, "How dare you, you inconsiderate, selfish brute!" Her neighbor acted as if he had no idea what she was talking about. She went on angrily, "You have the gall to deny that you left your trash all over my yard. Look at it. It's got your name on it. I'm sick and tired of your denial and your acting as if you are Mr. Innocent!" She slapped him across the face and twisted his arm behind his back. She woke up feeling wonderful and quite superior.

It was true that Caroline was very angry with her difficult neighbor, but he never actually had strewn trash across her yard, so she thought the dream might be metaphorical and she interviewed herself. First she asked herself to describe her neighbor and his behavior. She described him as a selfish, narcissistic, inconsiderate oaf who thought of himself as a kindly, often misunderstood middle-aged man. When she asked herself if this description reminded her of anyone in her life, she knew immediately that it reminded her very much of her husband and of his denial of responsibility for the difficulties in their marriage. She was shocked by her violence and the vehemence of her anger.

She also felt that her husband had indeed taken the trash of his own emotional life and spread it all over her life. She now thought it was time for him to clean up his own mess and grow up.

Maggot Man

Victoria had this dream the night after learning that her husband was having an affair: "My husband and I were in bed. He was sleeping and I woke him up. I sat him up in bed and proceeded to scream at the top of my lungs and tell him what a dishonest, untrustworthy, scheming, conniving, low-down, worm-ridden, maggot-infested person I thought he was. He was shocked.

"I woke up while my husband was sleeping beside me, and guess what? I actually woke him up and gave him a lively replay of my dream. I felt a lot better because the night before when I had found out about the affair, I was so shocked I couldn't even talk to him."

WHAT DO YOU SAY?

1. Describe why you are angry in the dream. Find three or four adjectives to describe how it feels to be angry in this particular way.
2. Describe the person at whom you are angry in the dream.
3. Does this description remind you of anyone in your life, or does it perfectly fit the person pictured in the dream?
4. How so? Elaborate to be sure you have made a good match.
5. Does the dream help you become more aware of stifled feelings of anger?
6. Are there tears underneath this anger?
7. What do you want to do about the anger you feel?

Being Pregnant or Giving Birth

VARIATIONS

In dreams both men and women can become pregnant and give birth. While women in their childbearing years are more likely to use these images in their dreams, men and women of all ages sometimes find these images express important issues in their lives. The dreamer may be happily pregnant or may be terrified that an unprotected sexual encounter has left her with an unwanted pregnancy. Some dreamers actually know that they have been pregnant for a particular number of months, and others know whether they are carrying a boy or a girl. Some dreams take one through breathing exercises and even the actual birth process. Pregnant mothers often dream of giving birth to deformed children. Luckily, these dreams are not predictive but rather are symbolic of the dreamer's anxieties and perhaps other conflicts.

WHAT OTHERS HAVE SAID

Jungians often interpret images of pregnancy and of birth as images representing the self or core identity and direction of the dreamer. Freud's discussions of birth issues in dreams centered around the fear of becoming pregnant or the hope of becoming pregnant. He felt that such concerns were represented not by literal pictures of birth and pregnancy but rather by metaphoric images such as the loss of a tooth or by images of babies coming out of various parts of the body or of babies coming out of or being rescued from bodies of water. He also interpreted as birth issues images of a bird bringing a gift, a message or a telegram arriving, and even water flooding into or out of a home or a building.

Our concern here is how to deal with dreams where the images themselves picture birth and pregnancy. Most modern dream analysts consider pregnancy and birth to be about something the dreamer is working on or developing. It might be a new part of himself or herself, a new project, a new company being developed by the dreamer, or also perhaps a new relationship. We have found it most useful to ask the dreamer to describe what it is like for him or her to be pregnant or to give birth and then to describe everything that is known about the dream situation. For example, if a woman dreams that she is three months pregnant, we might ask her, "What in your life has been growing for three months? Do you feel like you are giving birth to something new?" The dreamer then describes her feelings within the dream action and usually can bridge the dream to important issues in her waking life.

SAMPLE DREAMS

Corporate Babies

Paul dreamt: "I was in the emergency room giving birth to a huge baby. I was breathing in a Lamaze manner, pushing very hard, and all the while I had to fight off the doctors. There were just too many doctors, and they were interfering with the process."

In describing his feelings in the dream and the birth scene, Paul immediately bridged to the fact that he was giving birth to a company. He had to put forth enormous effort and was constantly being distracted by too many helpers, too many advice-givers. Just as in the dream, he felt he would do fine if he could get rid of the distracting intruders.

Expecting

Arlene dreamt: "I was two years pregnant, and I felt so heavy I began to worry the baby would never come."

Interviewing herself, Arlene asked, "What does it mean to be pregnant?" She responded that it means to give life, to prepare to give life to something new. She asked herself, "How do I feel that I've been preparing to give birth for two years and still feel that it hasn't happened?" Arlene bridged the dream to a job she had had for exactly two years, and she realized that she had been hoping that "next month" good things would start to happen. The dream made her feel that she might never have the baby at this job, that she might never be able to develop herself and find fulfillment in it. For two years she had been pregnant—an unnatural amount of time. If a mother were pregnant for that long, surely the pregnancy would fail. Arlene decided to find a new job and gave up hoping against hope that this one would work out for her.

WHAT DO YOU SAY?

1. Describe the pregnancy or the birth in your dream. Include the length of time of the pregnancy.
2. Is there anything in your life with which you feel pregnant that is reminiscent of the dream scene?
3. Describe any of the other people in your dream, including what they are like and specifically what their personalities are like. Do they remind you of any part of your life or anyone in your life?
4. Does the situation in the dream remind you of any situation in your waking life?
5. How so? Be specific; see if you have made a strong bridge.

Seeing Neglected or Mistreated Babies or Animals

VARIATIONS

In some very disturbing dreams, one notices babies or animals who have been neglected or starved or burned or in some way terribly abused. Sometimes the dreamer awakes after seeing them and feeling terrible for them; sometimes the dreamer wonders what to do and tries to figure out how to help the animals or whether it's too late to save them. Usually the dreamer awakens anxious and sad.

WHAT OTHERS HAVE SAID

Gestalt therapists believe that all images in dreams represent aspects of the dreamer. They see these images as neglected or misrepresented parts of the dreamer, perhaps suggesting childhood abuse, either physical or sexual, in which the child was terribly neglected emotionally or physically or was mistreated. Most therapists would agree that this is the most common interpretation for this dream, and I certainly agree. It is important for the dreamer to get a very careful description of the babies or the animals and of their condition. Often this brings tears to the dreamer's eyes. It is important for the dreamer to recognize the level of pain that is still buried within and that is making its appearance in the dream state.

SAMPLE DREAMS
Starved and Burned Little Kittens

Wendy woke up crying from this dream: "I looked behind a door in my room, and I saw these little kittens. They had been starved and grilled, burned. The hair was off, a lot of their skin was blistered, and they were just moaning in pain. They were so raw I could hardly stand it. I didn't know what to do, and I didn't know if it was too late to save them."

As she described the condition of the kittens, Wendy began to cry and vicariously feel their pain. I asked her, "Is there any part of yourself that feels like these kittens?" She burst into sobs. She said she was mistreated as a child, physically abused and emotionally neglected. She felt just as raw and burned as these kittens. I asked her, "What might have triggered this dream on this particular night?" She said she had had a family dinner the night before the dream, and being around her mother and father, trying to be happy and sociable, must have taken more of a toll on her than she had realized. She also saw that she had a lot more healing to do before she could fully recover from her terrible childhood.

Baby Boy Behind Desk

Joan dreamt that she saw a little baby boy behind her husband's desk at work. The child apparently had not been fed for days, nor had his diapers been changed. At first she was hesitant to take responsibility for the child because she didn't know whose child he was, but seeing that no one else was going to take care of him, she took him up in her arms, bathed him, and began to feed him. She felt uneasy about taking on this new responsibility in her life.

When she described the baby to her interviewer, Joan said that the baby was very much like her husband's feeling self. Her husband was a man who worked very hard, joked a lot, but was very out of touch with his feelings. It was as if he was afraid to know what he was feeling. She and her husband had just started couples' counseling, and Joan felt that she had to do most of the work in order to ease her husband into the experience of therapy. She bridged her feeling of taking on a whole new responsibility to her concern that she had begun to see how very undeveloped and immature her husband's feeling side is, and she began to wonder if she would have the patience to take care of him for the several years it would undoubtedly take him to develop emotionally into a more mature adult.

WHAT DO YOU SAY?

1. Describe the babies or the animals in your dream. Include anything you can say about how they feel and how you feel seeing them.

2. Is there any part of yourself or anyone in your life who is like this mistreated baby or animal?

3. What other feelings do you have in the dream? Do they parallel feelings you have regarding the person or part of yourself that is like the babies or animals?

4. How severely mistreated or neglected are these animals or babies? Do you or they need professional help to effect the healing?

Water Dreams

VARIATIONS

Whenever I give talks on dreams, either in lecture form or on television or radio, people are dying to ask what it means when you dream of water. This image is a perfect example of why old-fashioned dream symbolism with fixed meanings for particular images is a waste of time. Just think of different ways that water can appear in a dream. You might be in a beautiful bath, drowning in a violent sea, or saving a child from a polluted stream. You might be drinking from a romantic Hawaiian waterfall or sailing in the San Francisco Bay. The water could be pleasurable or frightening, romantic or sexy, and it could take forms such as tidal waves or rain or snow. You might water-ski or swim with dolphins, play with sea otters, or look down the throat of a humongous white shark. You could be washing clothes or dishes in fresh soapy water or maybe even cold greasy water.

WHAT OTHERS HAVE SAID

Obviously, water can mean an untold number of things depending on the dream and on how the dreamer feels about it. Meanings will also vary, of course, depending on who the dreamer is and how the dreamer chooses to use water as a symbol to express something important.

For psychoanalysts, water might represent the womb and a desire to return to the mother or to have intercourse with her. Jungians are fond of interpreting water as the unconscious with all of its frightening and rewarding but mysterious contents. Others interpret water as the spirit.

I think often water is used in a dream to provide one with the sensation of floating or with a fear of drowning or of being overwhelmed. Other dreams may bring the joyous experiences of swimming, feeling exhilarated, feeling taken care of, or magically enveloped. Sometimes water represents emotions, from stormy ones to placid ones to deep, meaningful ones. I think it is impossible to understand water imagery in dreams before describing the particular sort of water in your dream and your relation to it. If you do this carefully, you will know why you dreamt of it.

SAMPLE DREAMS

Water Rafting

Roger dreamt: "I was white-water rafting with a group of friends. The water was relatively calm, and then it started to pick up. Things started to get out of control; it got very rocky. The waters were going very fast, and I fell out of the raft into the water. I was losing consciousness. The water was very cold, I may have hit my head, and I wasn't sure that I would come back up again."

I asked Roger to describe the action in his dream and he said, "The most striking part of it was that everything seemed so calm and in control at first. Then the natural course of the river simply started to speed things up. I lost control and was afraid I would go under and die."

I asked Roger if these feelings reminded him of any situation in his life, and he responded that, yes, indeed, this is how he feels when he gets near drugs again and that in fact the people in the boat were friends he used to do drugs with. Currently he was off drugs and felt very in control. But in the last week he had started seeing some of these former drug friends again even though he wasn't using. Roger understood his dream to be pointing out to him how easy it would be to lose control, to fall back into his old habits and perhaps lose his life to his habit.

Esther Williams

Barbara dreamt: "I was in what felt like an Esther Williams production number. It was a huge swimming pool with fountains in it. I was wearing a beautiful bathing suit. There were lights, there was music. I was standing at the end of the pool, and there was a large audience at the other end. I knew my role. I was to dive into the pool with a beautiful swan dive and then join the others in a water ballet. I was very surprised in the dream that I wasn't anxious; in fact, I felt extraordinarily confident. I couldn't believe it. I felt a little anxiety but just the slightest bit. I dived into the pool, and it felt so wonderful. I felt like I had arrived somehow."

I asked Barbara, "Who is Esther Williams and what is she like?" She responded, "Esther Williams is a star from the forties who is elegant and very strong. She wasn't just a pretty star; she could swim. She had elegance, grace, and enormous strength. I admired her for this combination of qualities." I asked her if there was anyone in her life or any part of herself that was like Esther Williams. She laughed and told me that it took her forty-two years to come to a place in her life where she felt secure in her own sexuality and her own strength. Previously she had always felt that she had to choose to be either the pretty woman or the strong woman and that now she felt rather like Esther Williams. It was a very happy dream for her.

WHAT DO YOU SAY?

1. Describe the water in your dream.

2. Describe the action around the water in your dream. (Are you swimming, washing, water-skiing, watching a drowning?)

3. How do you feel in the dream? Be specific and describe your feeling with three or more adjectives.

4. If there are any people in your dream, interview yourself about each of them, using the questions in the section of this book called "People in Dreams."

5. If there are any major objects in the dream (boats, skis, buoys, bridges, and so forth), interview yourself using the questions in the section of this book called "Objects in Dreams."

6. Is there any situation in your life where you feel the way you do in the dream?

7. How does the dream action present a parable about a situation or a feeling in your current life?

8. How does the dream help you better understand this situation?

Dying or Being Killed in a Dream

VARIATIONS

Your dreams really get your attention when you actually die in them. You may die by your own hand, from an illness, or at the hand of an aggressor. Your death may be short and to the point—you may blow your brains out with a gun, or you may be executed. You may have a long dream with a complicated story line beginning with your being notified that you have a dreaded disease, then wasting away, and finally dying. A common myth is that if you fall in a dream and hit the bottom you must be dead and you will never wake up. Another myth is that if you die in a dream you will die in fact. Many people dream that they die, and the dream either ends there and the person wakes up or the dream continues in an often interesting and surprising manner.

WHAT OTHERS HAVE SAID

I feel strongly that interpretations suggesting that a dream of dying can be a healthy expression of yourself—of the dying of your old personality leading to a rebirth or a new sense of self—are not only misleading but dangerous. In my twenty years of experience working with people's dreams, I have never once seen this dream suggesting a healthy condition in the dreamer's life. On the contrary, a dreamer who is being killed, killing himself, or dying from disease is usually someone who is involved in self-destructive behavior or thought patterns or relationships. The people I know who have had those dreams, upon interviewing themselves, conclude that their dreams are red flags pointing put some area in their lives that is going terribly wrong.

SAMPLE DREAMS

Shooting Myself in the Head

Joshua dreamt: "I was standing somewhere, and I had a gun in my hand. I proceeded to shoot myself in the head and was amazed that I felt no pain."

I asked Joshua to pretend I come from another planet and to tell me why humans shoot themselves in the head. He said because they are usually in the depths of despair and want to end their lives. I asked him for a value judgment on that—what did he think about shooting himself in the head in general? Did he think this was a good idea for humans or not? He said, "Nope, it's a stupid way to solve your problems, but some people are driven to it. I certainly would never do it." I said, "It's interesting that you're doing it in the dream." He said that he felt no pain. I asked him, "Is there anywhere in your life that you feel despair and behave in a way to make yourself feel no pain even though you are doing something that is life-threatening to you?" For the first time, Joshua revealed to me that he had a serious cocaine habit. He said that he thought he had been shooting himself in the foot with his cocaine, but maybe he was really shooting himself in the head.

The Evil Chief of Police

Kayla dreamt: "I have been scheduled to be executed by a firing squad run by the evil chief of police, Scarpia. I'm trying to figure out what my crime was, and it had something to do with the fact that I had refused to do something the police insisted I do. I hadn't done anything wrong by my lights, but I hadn't followed their rules and regulations. As they were firing I awoke."

I asked Kayla, "What is an execution?" She said that a firing squad execution such as the one in the dream was not the result of due process of the law, but that it was a maneuver of strong-arm policemen who, once offended, can have anybody summarily shot. I asked her to describe Scarpia to me, and she responded that he was the evil chief of police of Rome in the Puccini opera *Tosca*. "What is Scarpia like?" I asked. She said, "An avaricious, control-crazy, sexually plundering, strong-arm, evil policeman. The phrase I remember best about him was that after he was murdered by Tosca, whom he had tried to plunder, she looked down at him and said, 'Before him all of Rome trembled.'" I asked Kayla, "Is there anyone in your life or any force or any part of yourself who is like Scarpia? Before whom all of Rome trembles, who is power crazy, and who, when offended, can have people summarily executed?" She said that was one picture, a very uncharitable one, of her husband, who, although he could be very kind and gentle, nevertheless had a streak in him as controlling and as vicious as Scarpia's. Indeed, her husband had the habit of scolding her mercilessly. This dream helped Kayla see and begin to contend more consciously with the Scarpia within her husband, with whom she was not dealing very effectively.

Had Kayla interpreted her dream as the beginning of the transformation of her personality, as something new and wonderful, I doubt that she would have been motivated to look at how much like Scarpia her husband was and how much work she had to do with herself and with her relationship before she could hope for any new life and new relationships to arise. The dream described the current situation; it did not promise a positive future.

1. Why are you dying or being killed or executed in your dream?
2. If there is one, describe the thing, agent, persons, or institution that is killing you.
3. Is there anything, any of your behaviors, or anyone in your life that is threatening your well-being that fits one of the above descriptions?
4. How so? Elaborate on the parallels; see if you've made a good bridge. If not, return to questions one and two.
5. What might you do in waking life to alter your situation?

Dreaming of the Dead

VARIATIONS

These are spooky dreams, sad dreams, happy reunion dreams: dreaming of the dead fascinates us all and brings great joy to many. You may dream of being with your deceased parents or mate or with a friend who died perhaps a very long time ago or just yesterday. These dreams can feel like normal ones and you only realize upon wakening that the person is dead. In other cases, when the deceased person appears you may immediately say to yourself, "Oh, this person is dead; how interesting that he or she is in my dream."

Often your task within a dream about a dead person may be that of recognizing and accepting the fact that this person is no longer with you in the waking world. Some very fortunate people dream of being reunited with their loved ones in a warm, powerfully real, unbelievably vivid way. They can awake from these dreams feeling as if they really were with the person they had loved and lost. These dreams don't feel like normal dreams; the encounters feel somehow much more like waking reality, in fact, sometimes even more real than waking reality. They have a distinctly different quality from other dreams, even from dreams in which the deceased appear but seem like any other character in a normal dream. From such reunion dreams some people awake crying, seeing the glass half empty, thinking, "How sad, how sad. I was just with my beloved husband, and now I have to wake, and he is not with me, and I will be sad and blue all day." Others are able to see the glass half full and think, "At least I had him for that moment, and I remembered vividly what it was like to be with him. Perhaps I was really with him."

WHAT OTHERS HAVE SAID

Whether or not we can have dreams that actually reunite us with the spirit of a lost one is a question no living person I know can answer, either in the affirmative or the negative. My interest is to help you make the best use of these experiences. Many ancient and classical dream interpreters, of course, interpreted such dreams literally, saying that the spirit of the dead person is truly there. Others, like Artemidorus, offered multiple interpretations of a metaphorical nature, depending upon the identity of the deceased and the deceased's relation to the dreamer as well as on the action that took place in the dream.

Most modern psychoanalysts agree that the image of a dead person in a dream usually represents some aspect of the dreamer's personality or someone important in the dreamer's life. A woman's dream of a dead mother may help in exploring feelings she still harbors regarding her mother or attitudes toward herself and her world inherited from her mother. Since the dead person in your dream could represent a part of yourself or anyone in your current life, it is important to describe the personality of the dead person first and then, and only then, look to see if that description bridges to someone in your current life or to some part of yourself.

The dreams of older people include greater numbers of characters who are deceased. This is logical for two reasons. First, many of the older person's friends may be dead, and so this cast of characters, who carry many meanings for him or her, will be drawn from the pool of friends who have already died. Also, older people make use of their dreams to begin preparing for death themselves, and the deceased people in their dreams, friends who have already made the transition, can serve as useful signposts or metaphors for the dreamer. If you dream of famous people who have died long ago, such as Abraham Lincoln or Martin Luther King Jr., you may use these characters to represent qualities in yourself or people in your current life, or they may well represent concepts, ideas, or ideals for which you understand the dream character to have stood. The fact that such figures are already dead may be irrelevant to your purpose in using them as metaphors.

Many traditional psychoanalysts believe the deceased in dreams almost always represent someone close to the dreamer, such as a father or a mother. While I think this is sometimes the case, often it is not, and the only way to find out, in my opinion, is to get a good description of the deceased person and then see what he or she relates to in the dreamer's life.

Some dreams of the deceased result in creative innovations. In a very famous example of a dream of a dead person, William Blake, who often dreamt of his brother Robert, reported that in a dream Robert gave him specific instructions for a unique technique to create Blake's luscious, colorful illustrations, a technique that only in the last decade has been rediscovered. In another example, a Mr. Fischer dreamt of a deceased gentleman, Mr. Hoffman, who in the dream presented an entire psychological technique to Mr. Fischer. The Fischer-Hoffman process has now become widely used in the United States to help people work through early parental conflict.

SAMPLE DREAMS

Hugs

Marla, at sixty-five years of age, had the following dream about her husband who had died three years earlier: "I dreamt I was sitting in the living room, when suddenly Jonathan walked in. He looked so healthy and happy. He put his arms around me, and we embraced. It was so wonderful to be with him; it was so real, it felt much more real than a dream. He said that he couldn't stay very long, he just wanted me to know that he loved me. Then the dream was over."

This is a common dream, and if the dreamer can take it with gratitude it can cheer her greatly. But if the dreamer is still in very deep mourning, these dreams tend to make her even sadder. I invite the dreamer to talk about her feelings and ask her how she would like to respond to the dream, and what is the best she can make of it. I tend to congratulate the dreamer and say, "Good for you that you are able to have that experience."

Didn't Wash the Car

Cynthia, in her early fifties, dreamt this dream about two years after her father had died: "I dreamt that my father came back to the house. It was very real, he was very present, but then he started to scold me and tell me that I had not washed the car lately and that I better get out there and do it right away."

When I asked Cynthia to describe the action in her dream and the scolding from her father, she immediately started to interpret, "Does this mean that he's angry with me and I shouldn't be going out with my friends and I certainly shouldn't think about dating?" I said, "I can't see any reason to jump to that conclusion. Let's first describe the action of the dream." She responded, "Well, in the dream my father is angry because I hadn't been cleaning the car, which is sort of silly." I asked, "What was your father's attitude toward car cleaning?" "Well, he always thought it was the right thing to do. One should always have a clean car. It was like being in your Sunday best." I asked, "What did he think of people who didn't clean their cars?" She said, "Probably they didn't care about appearance." "So, is there any way that if your father were alive now, he would be irritated with you for not caring about your appearance or getting the car cleaned?" She said, "Well, I'm not as active as I used to be, and ever since he died I don't want to go out much." When I asked her how she thought her father would feel about that, she said, "Oh, he might be a little bit irritated; I should get up and live life."

WHAT DO YOU SAY?

1. Describe the personality of the deceased person in your dream. Does this person, whom you describe as (restate the description), remind you of anyone in your life or of any part of yourself or of anything in your life?

2. How do you feel about this person?

3. What did the world lose when this person died?

4. How do you feel in the dream when you see this person?

5. What happens in the dream? What does the deceased person do or say, and how do you interact?

6. Does this remind you of any situation in your life?

7. How real did this dream encounter feel?

8. Why you think you might have dreamt this on this particular night?

Death of Someone You Care About

VARIATIONS

How awful it feels to wake up from a dream in which you have just witnessed or heard of the death of someone you love and care about! The distress can be very real, and it leaves some people worrying for days that the dream might come true. In fact, some people feel compelled to contact the person pictured in the dream to warn him or her that something terrible might happen. I would like to assure you that many people dream of the death of someone they love without that death coming to pass. I have listened to many, many dreams that never came true in a literal sense. While some reasonable people report they have dreamt of the death of a loved one at the same time that person died or within, say, a week or two of that person's death, I have yet to see this occur within my practice.

While in many dreams we feel terribly pained at the death, sometimes, surprisingly, the dreamer feels no grief and no sadness at all but simply accepts the death as fact. Within the dream the dear one's death may be reported verbally, it may be seen in the newspaper, or it may be heard on the radio. Or in what can be excruciating vividness, the dream may portray the accident or the death itself. These dreams merit the dreamer's attention because while, at least in most cases, they are not about what is going to happen, they are about what is going on in the dreamer's life at the time of the dream.

WHAT OTHERS HAVE SAID

Freud believed that the feeling of grief or the absence of it was an indicator of the meaning of the dream. For example, if the dreamer felt no grief at the death of a loved one, Freud believed that the death was simply a disguised hidden wish, a wish that itself would not cause any grief. I agree that the emotions felt or not felt in the dream are highly indicative of meaning. But I would argue that we can't know what that meaning is before eliciting good descriptions of the people, the actions, and the feelings in the dream.

The psychoanalyst Alexander Grinstein described cases in which patients dream of the death of a relative to express resentment or hostility toward that person. I have found that while many dreamers are shocked by this hypothesis, they nevertheless almost always consider this possibility. Sometimes such interpretations are accurate, but again I do not presume this is true. One should arrive at such a conclusion only after a careful interview. Freud believed that dreams of a loved one's death in which the dreamer experienced sadness and grief were expressions of wishes that the person in question would die. These wishes may stem from current circumstances or from early childhood. Again, while this may sometimes turn out to be an accurate interpretation, far more frequently dreamers who suffer such grief come to the conclusion that their dreams are about far greater concerns, hopes, and fears. Often the dead person represents a valued part of the dreamer's personality that may be dead, repressed, or somehow unavailable to the dreamer. The sadness the dreamer feels in the dream is often related to the dreamer's awareness, first recognized within the dream state, of a sadness over such a loss.

It may be that the deceased in the dream represents someone close to the dreamer whom the dreamer is currently undervaluing or treating in a way so destructive that the relationship itself may be threatened. If in describing the deceased person, the dreamer is reminded of someone who has actually died, it may be that the dream is helping the dreamer to grieve the loss and do emotional work that was left undone in the conscious state. Thus dreams can help us adjust to the loss of a loved one by helping us cry the tears we forbid while awake. In some dreams we use the death of someone we love to express our fears of abandonment and insecurity.

SAMPLE DREAMS

Mom or Sister or My Wife Dies
Benjamin had recurring dreams of the deaths of his mother, his sister, and his wife. These dreams would fill him with grief.

When Benjamin interviewed himself about a particular version of these dreams, he would describe the person who died and how he felt about it. He would discover in each case that his core feeling was one of abandonment. Only then did he notice that these dreams were precipitated by his wife's having to leave for business trips. The dreams helped him understand that his anxiety at the absence of his wife was connected to his fears of abandonment, which he had carried since childhood and which he had projected onto his mother, sister, and wife.

I Love You, Dad

Yet another possible use of the theme of the death of a loved one is represented by Rebecca's dream: "My deceased father appeared to me in a dream, and I finally had a chance to tell him how much I loved him. While he was alive I resented him so much for not being available to us and being cold to my mother. It wasn't until he died that I realized how hard he worked and how limited he was in his ability to express emotion. Now I wanted to tell him that I could forgive him for that and that I loved him and that I was sorry I had never said this to him while he was alive. I woke up relieved, as if I really had had a chance to tell him all this."

WHAT DO YOU SAY?

1. Describe the person who has died in your dream. Describe his or her major personality traits, both positive and negative, and any other unique features that pertain to this person.

2. What was the person doing in the dream?

3. How do you feel about that behavior? Is there anyone in your life besides the person actually pictured who fits this description?

4. If so, how so?

5. If the person pictured in the dream represents himself or herself, how does the dream action comment on your relationship with that person?

6. If the dream person represents someone else in your life or some part of your own personality, how does the dream action, including your feeling, shed light on your relationship to that person or to that part of yourself?

Dreams of War

VARIATIONS

War can be a harrowing experience even in dreams. We can play the role of a soldier, a military hero, or a hapless victim. We can find ourselves planning a war or piloting a plane and about to drop a bomb. We may be saving others from the ravages of war or simply taking shelter somewhere, waiting until it is over. In some dreams we worry about the aftermath of war. Some people dream of conventional warfare, some of medieval wars, and some of a third world war and full atomic glare.

WHAT OTHERS HAVE SAID

Jung and others, as well as I, note that dreams of war between two people, two countries, or two forces can symbolize conflicting beliefs, attitudes, or desires within the dreamer. Thus a man who is struggling in his job may dream of opposing forces in battle, one representing a part of himself that feels the need to stay in a boring job in order to provide for his family, and the other side representing his desire to liberate himself and start a new company no matter what the risk. People having moral conflicts and divergent desires often use war to clarify both the force and the identity of their conflicting desires and needs. Frequently, people use war scenes to express the pain of having had warring parents.

Most experienced therapists interpret dreams of war as having to do with personal or interpersonal conflict in a dreamer's life. Some New Age dream workers believe that World War III or Armageddon dreams may have a predictive element or make commentary on the planetary culture as a whole. In my practice, if I take the time to ask a dreamer to describe war as if describing it to someone from another planet and to describe the particular action of the dream, in every case the dream turns out to be about the dreamer's personal or interpersonal conflicts, often referring to warring parents or to a warring husband and wife. I have found that the planetary interpretations crumble when the dreamer is carefully interviewed. Such global interpretations usually serve to help the dreamer avoid confronting the real issues in his or her own life.

SAMPLE DREAM

Third World War

A California guru came to my office complaining of recurring dreams of World War III. He was quite sure that his dreams were predicting the future for humankind. I asked him to describe the exact nature of the war in his dream as if he were describing it to someone who had never heard of the concept of war. He said this was the third world war, a nuclear war that would be the end of life as we know it on earth. Everything we hold dear would be destroyed; all ecosystems as we understand them would be demolished. This war would be the result of humankind's lack of spiritual enlightenment.

I asked him how he felt in the dream. He said he felt painful conflict witnessing two sides fighting and holding back nothing—fighting with their worst weapons and ready to destroy absolutely anyone. I asked him if there were any part of his life right now or ever in his history that felt like a war where each side was willing to throw in its worst weapons and would hold back nothing to the point where the conflict was almost unbearable for him to stand. With great surprise he looked at me and said, "My parents used to fight like that. They were both alcoholics, and I was always worried that the next fight would be the last, that something terrible would happen. I didn't know what, maybe we would all die or something like that." I asked, "Is there anything going on in your life right now that might trigger these painful feelings?" He said he had started a new organization and had been appalled to see how much vicious fighting went on in his organization. He said he was worried that this fighting would ruin everything he had worked for so much of his life, trying to spread spiritual understanding and love in the world. He was a little reluctant to think that his dream could have such a mundane interpretation. But he said it certainly made sense that he would be as upset as he was in his current situation, because he was so sensitized to this kind of conflict as a child.

A personal, very particular interpretation is common for dreams of war. If you have such a dream, you will find that a careful dream interview will help you see what immediate practical application your dream might have to your life. You might be relieved to find that the source of your dream is not a future Armageddon but past trauma that is rearing its ugly head again in your adult life.

WHAT DO YOU SAY?

1. Describe the exact nature of the warfare in your dream. Describe it as if you were doing so for someone from another planet.

2. How do you feel during the dream action? Be as specific as you can; come up with at least three adjectives.

3. Is there any situation in your life, now or in the past, where you feel or have felt the way you do in the dream? For example, are you having a similar conflict, or do you remember past conflict with your family, battles between your parents, or conflict in your life now between you and your spouse, your friends, your co-workers?

4. Is there anything going on in your life right now that is like the war in your dream?

5. If the enemy is clearly identified in your dream, describe that enemy, its personality, goal, and motivation.

6. Is there anyone in your life or any force in your life that fits the description of your dream enemy?

7. Is the way the war is being conducted in the dream parallel to how you are conducting the conflict in your life? If so, would you like to, and can you, change that warfare?

Dreams of Aging

VARIATIONS

Our dreaming mind can help us prepare for and cope with the alarming experience of aging. In these dreams we somehow notice that we are getting older. We may look in the mirror and see signs of age, or we may dream of older people who are not coping well with the loss of youth. People who are particularly attached to a self-image that is young seem to report more dreams that picture surprise and dismay at aging. Some people end their dreams with a maturing acceptance, while others panic. Dreams of aging can take on almost any imagery. For example, a person who has been very involved with strenuous sports may start to have dreams of becoming a spectator rather than a participant. She can learn through a series of dreams to accept a new position that, although perhaps less exciting, can still provide many of the pleasures of the sport and of life.

WHAT OTHERS HAVE SAID

Dreams of aging are often misinterpreted as expressions of the fear of death, which they certainly can be but are not always. Most therapists recognize that an important task in growing up is that of accepting the aging process and the transitions from one stage of life to another.

SAMPLE DREAMS
White Hair

Halona dreamt: "I looked in the mirror, and I saw a number of white hairs and thought, 'Oh, I've got cancer.'"

When Halona interviewed herself, she described having white hair as one of the first signs of aging in humans. She described cancer as a deadly, wasting disease. She asked herself what in her life is like a cancer that is a deadly wasting disease. Halona was quite sure she was healthy, and she was quite sure that the white hair suggested her aging and losing her beauty. The dream helped her to reflect on her feelings about aging. She hadn't realized how deeply concerned she was about aging until she had this dream.

Yikes! Sagging Jowls

Veronica dreamt that she was looking in the mirror and noticed that the skin at her jowls was beginning to sag. She was shocked that at the age of thirty such a thing could be happening to her. She didn't like the look and yet she said, "This is inevitable. If I'm lucky enough to live, this will happen to me. Maybe it's already beginning to happen and I haven't even noticed it."

This was a fairly transparent dream for Veronica. She said it was her first inkling she would lose her beautiful face and that within the dream itself she was practicing accepting the inevitable.

WHAT DO YOU THINK?

1. Describe the indications of aging in your dream.
2. How do you feel in the dream about this aging?
3. How do most humans feel about aging? Why do they care?
4. Are you more worried about losing your youth than you have recognized?
5. What role does your concern about aging play in your major relationships and in your sense of yourself both at work and at home?

Finding Money

VARIATIONS

What a delightful surprise to find money in a dream! You may find other valuables, such as priceless paintings hidden in an attic, beautiful jewelry you didn't know you had, or even a car you didn't know was yours. The money may be in the sand, or you may find it under your pillow, under your mattress, in a closet, or in an old coat you haven't worn for years. Some people find money in a dream and happily take it without any conflict, assuming it was theirs or was there for the taking. Others see money and don't dare touch it, thinking it must belong to someone else.

WHAT OTHERS HAVE SAID

In 200 C.E. Artemidorus wrote, "Some men maintain that money and all kinds of coins indicate bad luck but I have observed that small coins and copper coins mean discontent and painful exchanges of words. Silver coins symbolize discussions that involve contracts about important matters; gold coins, about matters that are even more important. It is always better to have just a few coins and not much money rather than a great deal since a large amount of money signifies anxieties and griefs because it is difficult to manage. This is also true of treasure. "If a man finds that he finds a treasure that contains only a little money, it signifies that the hardships will be smaller."[7] These are amusing metaphors, but can you imagine using money to represent such meanings in your dreams?

I am sorry to tell you that although many people have interpreted dreams of finding money as foretelling an inheritance or financial fortune, my experience does not bear this out. In fact, I have never seen a money dream that foretold the future in a literal way. But the good news is that almost all dream analysts agree that finding money has to do with the dreamer's discovery of new and positive qualities and potentials within herself or himself.

SAMPLE DREAMS

Finding Money in the Sand

Dineen dreamt: "I was walking along the beach enjoying the sunlight and sunset, just feeling good about the world. It seemed as if I had just recovered from some difficult time and I was feeling rested and healthy again, when I noticed coins in the sand. Nickels and quarters here and there. I thought I had come upon a little treasure. As the dream ended I was collecting the coins and putting them in my pocket."

Dineen described her treasure as a happy, lucky find. As a child she had always enjoyed finding coins in the sand. She felt that fortune was smiling upon her in the dream. I asked her if her dream feeling of being lucky and finding good fortune after having had a difficult time and now recovering reminded her of any situation in her life. She said, "Oh, yes! I have just gone through a terrible divorce, and I think the healing process has gone far enough for me to feel good about living again. In the dream, even though I don't find much money, that's not a problem. The feeling of being lucky and having little pleasures here and there reminds me of how my life seems to be now. Filled with good friends—even some nice men. I just feel like I'm walking at the sunset of my life, at the late afternoon of my life, really, and having a very nice time. Four years ago I would have never dreamt this was possible."

The Gold Maserati

Roberto dreamt: "I went to clean out my garage, and as I started throwing out boxes and other debris I got to the back of the garage, which in the dream was very large, and I found a beautiful gold Maserati sports car. But the most amazing thing was that I realized that someone had left this car here for several years and it was in perfect condition. Then somehow I just understood that the car was mine and I had forgotten that I had it. I couldn't believe that I could have forgotten such a thing, nor could I believe my good fortune. I couldn't wait to take the car out for a spin."

Asked to describe a gold Maserati to someone who had never seen such a thing before, Roberto said, "It is the crème de la crème, the best and most exciting of all the cars in the world. It has beauty, grace, and wonderful functionality and power." I asked Roberto if there was anything in his life or any part of himself or anyone in his life who was like a gold Maserati, powerful, beautiful, the crème de la crème, the most exciting car possible, that he had also been unaware of for the last several years or had forgotten that he had. Roberto replied that if he were to drop all modesty he would say, "I have energy like that. At least I used to, but I have been working so hard for the past few years that I haven't been having much fun, and this car is definitely a car to have fun in. I have just retired, and I've been very worried about retiring. If this dream is any indication, maybe I'll be able to reconnect with my Maserati energy— a sense of freedom and beauty and power—and live life as it should be lived. Yes, that must be it, because in the dream I had time finally to clean out the garage, and I knew that when I retired I should spend some time and clean out the garage. Wow, what a great dream!"

WHAT DO YOU SAY?

1. Describe the money or valuables you find in the dream.

2. Where do you find them?

3. Is there anything in your life that is like the money or valuables that you find in your dream which you describe as (restate the description)? How so?

4. Does the place you find your treasure suggest any area of your life that holds riches or opportunities for you?

5. Describe in as much detail as you can the parallels between your dream valuables and the strengths, skills, or opportunities in your life you think they represent.

6. Why do you think you had this dream at this particular time in your life?

Arriving at an Important Decision

Sometimes in a dream we come to a very clear decision about actual situations in our waking lives. The decision may show itself in metaphorical or literal terms. For example, you may decide which of two or three people you want to go off with in a dream. You may decide in a dream that you are so angry at someone that you call off the relationship. Or you may decide to marry someone in a dream or make a career change or initiate a creative project. When you make a clear decision in a dream, it is wise to ask yourself whether or not the decision seems a good one in the light of waking consciousness. Decision dreams can be turning points in your life, but it is important to interpret them carefully.

WHAT OTHERS HAVE SAID

In two decades of being particularly curious about decision dreams, I have been fascinated to see that people make wise, reckless, foolish, and often just plain terrible decisions in dreams. It is very important in these circumstances that dreamers ask themselves to judge the quality of the decision made in the dream using good common sense in the waking state. I have noticed many times that decisions made in dreams, viewed from a waking perspective, are really stupid decisions. In these cases it is important to interpret the dream metaphorically, asking yourself how you might be in the process of making an unwise decision. For an example, see my dream "Sentenced to Solitary Confinement" under the "Prisons" entry in chapter 3, "Dream Settings."

SAMPLE DREAM

Anna Drinks; It's Over

After having been to a dinner party with his wife, Anna, at which she had drunk too much and then asked him if he would mind if she had yet another drink, Sergio dreamt: "We are on our way to a party. My wife, Anna, is sitting in the back seat of the car, and I am driving. She asks about having more to drink, perhaps another glass. I know that will be too much. I turn and ask her, 'Anna, do you really want to know how I feel when you get altered by having too much to drink, more than every once in a while, that is?' She says, 'Yes, I want to know.' Well, I really tell her. 'It repulses me. It infuriates me. I find you get boring and repetitive, and I wish I were not with you.' Then Anna complains to the others in the car that I only let her have one small cup of wine, making me look like an unreasonable policeman. I suddenly say, 'That's it! Now you're turning this into a public affair. It's all over, I'm leaving for good. I will not put up with the drinking or all the nonsense that goes on around it anymore.'"

Sergio knew immediately upon awakening that he had expressed what was deep in his heart, his incredible anger and the fact that he was thoroughly repulsed by his wife when she was drinking too much. He decided to talk to his wife about her drinking in the morning and tell her that he was no longer willing to play her policeman or even to be around her when she had more than a couple of drinks in the evening. It would now be up to her to decide what she wanted to do with her drinking. He would be leaving her if she did not change her behavior drastically within the next couple of weeks. He was very happy with his decision. When Sergio really expressed how he felt, the decision he had to make was clear.

WHAT DO YOU SAY?

1. Describe the decision you make in your dream.
2. What led up to your making the dream decision? For example, it was only after Sergio really expressed how repulsed he felt and after his wife had made it a public affair that his decision was made.
3. How wise is your decision in the dramatic context of the dream?
4. How wise is the decision in the context of your waking life?
5. Has your dream opened your eyes to something you really should have realized earlier?

Discovering New Rooms in a House

VARIATIONS

Almost every time I give a lecture or talk about dreams on radio or television, someone in the audience wants to tell me about a dream of entering a familiar or an unfamiliar house and discovering more or new rooms. The dreamer's face lights up, and even without knowing what the dream means specifically, he or she understands something good is going on. The new rooms are often filled with sunlight and fresh air, and the dreamer is amazed to discover that all these extra rooms exist. Now and then the new rooms discovered are in need of repair, but the dreamer almost always feels hopeful and confident of being able to fix them up and make them look wonderful. Very often the dreamer is aware of having known the house well but never having realized that the house had all this room in it. These dreams usually carry feelings of happy surprise and optimism for the future.

WHAT OTHERS HAVE SAID

Freud, in his rigid, sexist classical psychoanalytic style, saw houses as representing bodies. The stairs were symbols of intercourse, the open doors were vaginas and other orifices, balconies were breasts, water pipes the urinary tract, and so forth. He wrote, "Rooms in dreams are usually women; if the various ways in and out of them are represented this interpretation is scarcely open to doubt." Elsewhere he wrote, "A dream of going through a suite of rooms is a brothel or harem dream."[8] Jung and most of his followers suggest a broader range of possible interpretations according to the context of the dream. In general, most psychotherapists today consider a house as capable of representing a dreamer's lifestyle, marriage, emotional state, or a particular time in the person's life indicated by the period of time in which the dreamer lived in the house. Regarding the finding of new rooms, most dream analysts would consider this a likely representation of the dreamers' discovery of new parts of themselves, new potentials within their personalities, and/or new areas to explore or to refurbish that have previously been ignored. I have noticed that such dreams often signal recent progress on the part of the dreamer in discovering a fuller sense of life or a fuller sense of self.

SAMPLE DREAMS

More Rooms

Pasquale dreamt: "I am walking through a familiar house and discovering new rooms on the left, new rooms on the right. They are big, beautiful, and flooded with sunlight. I am so amazed; I had no idea that these rooms were here all the time. I am delighted to think I have this much space and shocked that I hadn't realized this before."

Pasquale had this dream within the year that he had decided to retire from an extremely workaholic lifestyle. He had begun to suspect that there might be more to life than working and achievement. He was beginning to get interested in the arts, sports, and deeper relationships with women. He wanted to travel. He interpreted the house as a representation of himself and of large spaces within himself he had not previously enjoyed. All that remained now in the dream was for him to furnish the rooms, to live in these rooms, and to use the space. The feeling was one of expansiveness and delight in discovering new space, new possibilities.

Room with Potential

Gia dreamt: "I was walking through my house, and I discovered a corridor that I had not realized existed. I went into the rooms off the corridors, and I was amazed to see how very big they were. One in particular was a bedroom that was huge and had lots of potential, but it looked to be in serious need of repair. Parts of the walls were peeling, windows had been broken, and it was pretty messy. Nevertheless, it wouldn't take too much work to make it a beautiful, lovely, romantic bedroom. I was very happy when I woke up."

Gia described the bedroom as a place that had been boarded up for a long time after having been seriously trashed, just as she had been sexually abused as a child. The bedroom had to do with her sexual self, one that she had boarded up for a long time and now, in therapy, was repairing. This room had the potential to be beautiful and romantic and to provide her a space in life for her sexuality. She was happy to note that it had always existed and that now she could repair and refurbish it.

WHAT DO YOU SAY?

1. Describe the house in your dreams.
2. Does it remind you of any particular house in your life?
3. Describe the new room or rooms you discover.
4. Does this room have a particular purpose?
5. How do you feel about this room?

6. Are you discovering new parts of yourself or of your life that you would describe as (restate the descriptions of the house and room or rooms)?

Finding New Talents or Qualities You Didn't Think You Had

VARIATIONS

What a surprise it is to dream that suddenly you can sing beautifully when in waking life you can hardly carry a tune! Many sports people dream of executing their sport with skill far beyond their waking-level achievement. Golfers drive balls as if they were Jack Nicklaus; ice skaters, like myself, who can achieve only a single-axel jump in the waking state, in dreams can easily jump huge, beautiful double and triple axels. Dancers can dance like magic, and musicians and poets create pieces of exquisite beauty. Sometimes we are able to sing or dance or run with the very best in the field and we are accepted as equals; at other times we are able to express feelings more deeply, achieve insights more gracefully than ever we could while awake. In fact, one of the most precious qualities of dreaming is that it offers us our first opportunity to experience firsthand new levels of intimacy, joy, compassion, love, and peace of mind that can immeasurably enrich our waking experience of living. When people tell me they rarely remember their dreams I think to myself, "How sad that these people have no idea what they're missing."

WHAT OTHERS HAVE SAID

In my twenty-year practice of working exclusively with people's dreams, I have found dreams of new talents or skills to be among the sweetest of all. If we use these dreams wisely, they can facilitate quantum leaps in personal development. The sport, the art, or the feeling tone that the dreamer achieves acts as a beacon showing what is possible, at least on a metaphoric level. The sport and art dreams usually provide a big boost to the dreamer's self-esteem and motivation, sometimes acting as a pat on the back, as if to say, "You're doing well." Other times the dreams give clues about what might be holding the dreamer back from such achievement or about what could help the dreamer move forward. Sometimes a sport is used as a metaphor for life in general. When the dreams deal with introducing the dreamer to new states of feeling, to new abilities and depths of loving, understanding, and joy, the dreamer can then look at his or her life and ask important questions, such as, What keeps me from feeling this way while I am awake? and, What do I need to do in my life to encourage these feelings and these ways of being? To call these dreams wish fulfillments only would be to neglect the motivating power of the firsthand experience that comes in these dreams. The teaching potential of these dreams is great: they show you what it *feels* like to do something extremely well.

SAMPLE DREAMS

Triple Axels!

I once dreamt that I was ice skating and practicing my axel jump, which is one and a half revolutions in the air. As I was taking off for the jump, a voice within me said, "Don't worry about the landing while you're taking off; just think about jumping into the air." I would practice this attitude, which of course made my takeoff bigger, freer, and less constricted. My jump worked perfectly, and I thought, Well, that was so easy, why don't I try a double axel (two and a half revolutions)? I realized that if I managed not to be afraid while taking off, I could achieve the revolutions and land smoothly. Well, I thought, if that was easy, why don't I just try a triple! What a thrill—three and a half revolutions in the air, and I landed like a bird!

I woke up in the morning and realized that my ice skating was a metaphor for life. If I restrict myself with fear as I take off into a new adventure, then my landing is likely to be shaky. But if I just pay attention to my technique, taking off well—carefully but with courage—a much more exotic, exhilarating life would be mine. Later that day when I actually went ice skating my single axels were a lot better because my takeoff was much cleaner. My doubles and triples, however, were left to my dreams.

Great Lover

Gary dreamt: "I was in bed with my wife, and while I usually feel somewhat impatient during foreplay, in the dream I was exquisitely pleasured by giving her pleasure, and as I looked into her eyes I felt a depth of intimacy and love I'd never known before. It was a truly magical moment."

When Gary described the feelings in his dream, he said that his heart felt more open than he had ever thought possible. He felt a kind of generosity and love toward his wife that was more mature, rich, and overflowing than anything he had experienced previously. He told his wife this dream when he woke up, and he tried to kiss her and hold her and be with her in the way he was with her in the dream. He found he could recapture almost all of the magic of the dream. His wife, needless to say, was overjoyed.

WHAT DO YOU SAY?

1. Describe the new talents or feelings you discover in your dream.

2. Describe, as specifically as you can, the feelings you experienced.

3. Are there any clues in the dream that could be metaphors for obstacles to attaining this level of achievement or this depth of feeling? Could the clues be showing you how to encourage this feeling in your waking life?

4. If you are dreaming of a new sport or talent or art form, could this be a metaphor for your whole life or for certain attitudes or ways of being in your life?

5. Could this dream be a straightforward motivational experience for you regarding your particular sport or art form?

6. For the next three days, try to think often of this dream and become very familiar with the wonderful feelings it engenders in you. Make these feelings part of your life.

Visiting Your Childhood Home

VARIATIONS

Many of our dreams of childhood take place in the home or in one of the homes we grew up in as children. Often the house is very vivid in the dream, and it seems quite natural that we should be there again. Usually, but not always, we return to the house as an adult and some drama or encounter takes place there. Usually the house seems to be as it was when we last knew it; however, sometimes the house appears to be rundown or refurbished. The people we encounter in our house in the dream may be those from our childhood or from our present life, or they may be strangers.

WHAT OTHERS HAVE SAID

While orthodox psychoanalysts tend to see dreams of childhood homes as a form of emotional regression concerning early life and parental issues, modern psychoanalysts and most modern dream analysts consider such a setting capable of representing a wide variety of meanings. In general, the dream will concern itself with issues in your life that were active or began during the period in which you lived in that house. Often these concerns or conflicts have to do with childhood and parental issues that you have carried forward into adult life. For example, if you dream of being back in your High Street house that you lived in between the ages of ten and fifteen, you would look at the feelings and situations of that time in your life to discover the matter the dream is treating. The characters and their behavior will help you target the specific meaning of your dream.

SAMPLE DREAMS

Bickering at Home

Mark dreamt: "I'm back at the 434 Chestnut Street house. We are in the kitchen, and my father has just come home from work. My girlfriend and I have come for dinner, and we are helping Mom set the table. My father has gone into the living room to read the paper, and my mother is calling him to come in and help. They bicker. I wonder how they can live like this."

When I asked Mark to describe how he felt about the dream scene, one he remembered occurring repeatedly in his childhood, he said that even though he was an adult in the dream he felt trapped, that his parents were still up to their old tricks. Mark's parents had died several years earlier, but the dream vividly brought back those feelings and memories. I asked him if there was anything going on in his life right now that felt like being back home listening to his parents bicker about who was being lazy and who was working hard. Mark responded that he was not reliving such a circumstance; in fact, he was particularly glad not to be married because he didn't want to re-create that kind of bickering in his adult life. He added, "My girlfriend wants us to live together, and I've been very reluctant even though I like her a lot. I think the dream really does target one of my major resistances to living with someone. I just don't want to be part of the bickering that is an integral part of so many marriages."

I Can Dance

Emma dreamt: "I was back at the home I lived in during high school years, and there was a big party going on. I was having fun being with my friends and dancing, but I couldn't find my boyfriend. I looked for him here and there but finally decided that if he wanted to he could come back to the party, find me, and we could dance."

I asked Emma to describe how it used to feel to be in the house. She said it was a very happy time in her life. "I went to a wonderful high school, I was very popular and had lots of parties." I asked, "Does anything going on in that house remind you of anything in your life right now?" Emma said, "No, actually, I haven't felt that way in years." I asked her, "In the dream you can't find your boyfriend, so you decide to stop looking for him. Does that remind you of any situation in your life, perhaps with your boyfriend?"

Emma said, "Oh, yeah, it sure does. My boyfriend is a very quiet, reflective sort of fellow, and he doesn't take partying seriously enough. He thinks it's frivolous and unnecessary, so for several years I've let that part of my life wither away. You know, in the dream I really was willing to say okay, you can come to the party or not, but I'm going to dance. I believe that's more the attitude I have to take with my boyfriend because I really miss the kind of fun I used to have when I was in school at home."

WHAT DO YOU SAY?

1. Describe the home you picture in your dream. What was your life like, and how did it feel to be in that home in those days?

2. How did it feel to be at the home in the dream?

3. Do these feelings remind you of anything in your current life?

4. How so?

5. What was the dream action at your home?

6. Who were the main people in the dream?

7. Describe each one and see if they remind you of something in your current life.

8. Do the feelings of your childhood home in this dream and the people and the action in it remind you of current feelings or situations in your life?

9. How so?

10. How does seeing the parallel to your childhood experience shed light on your present life circumstances?

Examination Dreams

VARIATIONS

There you are, frantically looking for the right room, about to take an exam for which you are totally unprepared. The test may be terribly important, such as the bar exam or the graduating exam from a school system, or it may be relatively unimportant, such as one course in a college curriculum. The test may take the form of a high school test, a doctoral exam, performing lines in a play, or singing an aria in an opera. The test may be reciting one's lines at a bar mitzvah or confirmation ceremony. The test may be illegible or on the wrong topic, or perhaps you forgot to study all term. Or there you stand on stage, everyone is waiting for you to sing, but you can't remember a single line. You wake up at that terribly anxious moment relieved it was only a dream. Sometimes the dreamer who is struggling with an exam or a karate test realizes that he has already passed this test, perhaps years ago. Why is he struggling through it again? An amusing variation is one in which the dreamer is about to take a test, realizes he hasn't studied and is unprepared, but decides to take the test anyway since he couldn't do worse than getting an F. He does not wake up until he has found out that he got an A on the exam! You can imagine how this common dream with its many variations can have very many different meanings.

WHAT OTHERS HAVE SAID

Freud had a very convoluted explanation for examination dreams, which I will try to present briefly. He noted that these dreams usually occur just before the dreamer has to face some challenge or test in life for which he must be responsible and perform well. While dreaming, the individual finds an occasion in the past, such as an exam that he has already passed, and shows himself that his anxiety is unjustified since he succeeded before this in a similar endeavor. Thus the dream can be seen as a consolation. The anxiety, which the dreamer attributes to the dream, Freud believed constituted a concealed self-reproach for "reprehensible sexual acts."[9] Grinstein and other contemporary psychoanalysts interpret the anxiety in examination dreams as being related to fears of punishment and failure of a sexual nature. Grinstein also believes that in certain cases the dream should be interpreted by assuming that it is really the dreamer asking the difficult questions of the adult. Thus the dream disguises a turn of tables on the adult "who did not enlighten him about sexual matters for he [the dreamer] is now the knowledgeable examiner and they are ignorant and childish." Grinstein also writes that in dreams having to do with physical or anatomical exams there is often reference to "the dread that by the examination the doctor will discover that the patient had masturbated and will divine from this his particular fantasies and punish him severely; castration, humiliation, rejection, abandonment etc."[10] Most contemporary analysts take a much more direct approach to examination dreams.

At our dream center we look to see if the dream comes the night before an actual test, and if so, we ask the dreamer, "Are you prepared or unprepared for the test?" You may be well prepared and simply overly anxious. Some dreamers are such perfectionists, so anxious about winning approval from the people around them, that no matter how well prepared they are for an actual test in life they are unable to develop an appropriate level of confidence. This in itself indicates work to be done on self-esteem and perfectionism issues.

Next we ask the dreamer to describe the circumstances of the examination and to explore the possibility that the exam could act as a metaphor for tests in the dreamer's life or for a sense of being tested or examined. The specific details of the dream then can offer clues to the area in life with which the dreamer is contending, and may also offer a picture of the dreamer's mode of coping under examination pressure. If the dreamer has this dream frequently, it is important to consider whether or not the dreamer is living a life with so many deadlines and so many demands that she realizes she is never fully prepared, never able to really keep up. If the dreamer within the dream begins to protest the unfairness of the exam—that it is illegible or on the wrong topic—the interviewer would ask for good descriptions of the test givers to see who or what they represent in the dreamer's life. If the dreamer copes well, saying that he is unprepared and would like to take the exam later, or if the dreamer chooses to go ahead and take the exam anyway just to see what's possible, this could indicate that the dreamer is beginning to learn how to cope either with a too busy or too demanding lifestyle or with his own needs to succeed. It may indicate also that the dreamer is beginning to take responsibility for her own procrastination or lack of preparation for life's challenges, be they specific tests or encounters with people in her career or private life.

SAMPLE DREAMS

Crazy Exam

Charlie dreamt: "I am supposed to take a test in one of my courses in high school, but I can't find the room where the exam is supposed to be given. I look all over. I arrive about ten minutes late and pick up the exam, but it doesn't make any sense to me. Either the writing isn't clear or it's the wrong language, but I'm not going to be able to take the exam."

Charlie, a member of one of my dream study groups, told us, "The funny thing about this exam dream is that I'm sure I was prepared, but the school had put it in the wrong room. I don't think it was my fault, and furthermore, the exam wasn't legible. It wasn't at all what I had prepared for." An interviewer asked Charlie, "Well, then, whose fault was it that you were in such a predicament?" Charlie said, "It had to be the school's fault." He felt responsible in the dream, but, in fact, he was not and he was being tested unfairly. Asked where in his life he felt he was being tested unfairly, where obstacles were being put in his way and where there was a bait and switch, he said, "My whole life I've felt like that. I could never please my father; he was always testing me. He was always testing me beyond my abilities as if he were playing games with me. In school I always tried to show him that I could do well, but even when I did he'd always have another test for me." The interviewer asked him, "Why do you think you had this dream recently? Is there anything going on in your life now that reminds you of these feelings and of these circumstances?" Charlie responded that his job feels like that. He trains for one activity, masters it, and the next thing he knows he is transferred to a higher level but is expected to perform well immediately. This dream helped Charlie see how he was continuing a lifestyle he had started as a child. As an adult he was not taking options to manage his life better. His unsatisfied need for approval was getting in his way.

Forgotten Exam

Alvin dreamt: "I'm in a classroom and am about to take an exam on English poetry when I realize that I had forgotten to study over the weekend. In fact, I had watched football all weekend, and I had forgotten all about the exam. I woke up with a start because I knew this was an important test. Without it I would not graduate from high school."

Alvin was asked to describe English poetry. He said, "My wife loves it a lot. It's beautiful and romantic, but I don't really know very much about it. It's all right, I guess." When asked to describe football he said, "Oh, that's just fun. Guys really like that stuff a lot, and I really love the game." His interviewer asked, "Are you feeling that you have to be tested on something that's romantic and that your wife really loves, but you've been spending your time watching football with the guys?" Alvin just laughed and said, "Well that's pretty obvious, isn't it? My wife has actually put me on notice that if I don't become more attentive and romantic with her she is either going to take a lover or leave me."

WHAT DO YOU THINK?

1. Is there any actual exam or test you are about to take for which this dream could express anxiety?

2. Are you prepared or not for the actual exam, and is the dream a realistic concern or an exaggerated expression of your insecurity?

3. Describe the kind of test or challenge you are being confronted with in the dream as if you were describing it to someone from another planet.

4. What goes wrong in the dream? Are you ill prepared? Is the test illegible?

5. Do you have any idea why you are unprepared?

6. Is there any situation in your life that feels like you are being tested in the way you are in the dream and for which you are unprepared for the same reasons you have just stated?

7. Taking the larger view on this dream, do you think you have overly perfectionistic need based on insecurity to pass exams and in fact put yourself in too many testing situations? If so, is there anything you would like to do about it?

8. If you understand your dream to be reminding you of how you are in fact unprepared for a life challenge or an actual test, what might you do now or before your next test to be better prepared?

Forgetting Lines in a Play

VARIATIONS

See "Examination Dreams," above. Forgetting lines in a play usually has the same significance as examination dreams, but these dreams, of course, are more frequently suffered by actors and singers. The same issues are usually involved. If the dreams come very frequently they suggest either too heavy and demanding a schedule, or they suggest that the dreamer has not developed enough self-confidence to thrive in this lifestyle because deep down the dreamer still feels inadequate, incompetent, and criticized.

Using a Phone That Doesn't Work

VARIATIONS

There you are trying to get through to your girlfriend or boyfriend, or, worse yet, your car is broken down and you have to call for help, or someone is about to attack you and you have to call for help. You get to the telephone—and it won't work. Either the telephone malfunctions, or you don't have the right change to put into it, or you are dialing the emergency 911 number and the operator is totally uncooperative. You wake up frustrated and sometimes frightened.

WHAT OTHERS HAVE SAID

Most modern analysts agree that in general dreams of a phone that won't work suggest a failure in communication. If the dreamer is trying to ask for help, then it makes sense to ask if the dreamer is in a difficult physical, financial, or emotional situation and is unable to communicate his need for help either to the people he is immediately involved with or to professionals. If the dreamer is unable to get through to a loved one on the phone, then one looks to see if there is trouble in communication between the dreamer and that particular person or the person represented by the dream character. If the dreamer doesn't have the proper change to make the connection, this could also suggest that the dreamer is unprepared or does not have the resources or perhaps the communication skills necessary to be in emotional connection with the person she is trying to reach. If the dreamer is able to contact people who would normally be able to help him, say workers at the 911 number, but these workers are uncooperative and frustrate his needs, then we ask if the dreamer is asking the wrong people in his life to help him out of a particular situation. It could be that the dreamer has an incompetent psychotherapist or marriage counselor and needs to find better assistance.

SAMPLE DREAMS

No Answer

For about a month Luigi had the following dream: "I am telephoning my girlfriend, Sophia, but there is no answer. I wake up frustrated and worry that maybe this dream means she is seeing another man."

When I interviewed Luigi I said to him, "Pretend I come from another planet. What does it mean on earth when you telephone someone and there is no answer?" He said, "Well, it could mean the phone is out of order. It usually means the person isn't home, and the person could be doing anything." I asked him, "In the dream do you worry that she is out with another man?" He said, "No, I think I worry about that when I wake up. In the dream I'm just frustrated that she is not there." I asked him if there was any way in the last month that Sophia had not been there for him. He said, "You bet! Sophia's mom died this month, about a month ago, in fact, and she has been very busy with that and very busy with her work. She has had no time for me, and I feel that she hasn't been there for me. Now that I look at this dream I realize it's time for me to stop worrying about myself and my needs and stop assuming the worst. It's time for me to help her deal with her mom's death. I guess I've been pretty selfish, haven't I?"

911 Equals 411

Alicia dreamt that her car had broken down on a country road. She walked to a telephone feeling a little anxious and dialed 911, but the information service, 411, answered, so she tried again and again. Information answered each time. She woke up frustrated and anxious.

In our interview I asked Alicia to pretend I come from another planet. I asked, "Tell me, why do humans call 911?" She said, "You call them for emergency help when you are in dire straits. I was in some danger out on this road by myself." "What is 411?" I asked. She replied, "That is the information service. While those people can put you in touch with other numbers, they don't actually do the helping; they are a referral service." I asked Alicia, "Is there anywhere in your life where you feel anxious or stranded and you think you've been calling for help but you are really dialing 411, a referral service, an information service?" She said that could be a description of her marriage counselor. She added, "I need help with my marriage. I think I need help to get out, but I've been working in therapy more in an information-gathering way. I'm a psychologist myself, and my therapist and I have not been taking my situation seriously enough. Acting too intellectual, gathering information rather than taking action. That's it, that's what I've been doing."

WHAT DO YOU SAY?

1. Describe the situation in your dream. Does the phone malfunction? Do you have the right change or credit card? Are you unable to get through to someone?

2. Can you describe the person or organization you are trying to get through to?

3. Does this person or organization, which you describe as (restate the description), remind you of anybody in your life, or is it an actual picture of the person you need to communicate with?

4. How so? Elaborate on the connection if you see one.

5. Why do you want to get through to this person or group?

6. What are the obstacles? Does this obstacle, which you describe as (restate the description), remind you of anything in your life?

7. Does this dream describe any difficulty you are having in waking life communicating with a particular person or asking for help in a particular situation?

8. How so?

9. If you don't have the right change to make the call, does this remind you of any way in which you are ill equipped to make effective communication with the person or persons in question?

Trying to Find a Private Toilet

VARIATIONS

Talk about embarrassing dreams! What could be worse than having to go to the bathroom and not being able to find a private place to do it? You may be in the middle of the street, sitting on a toilet without any enclosure around it, or you may be visiting someone's home when a party of people walk into the bathroom while you are seated there. Usually the others, the spectators who are the witnesses in the dream, are remarkably unconcerned about your predicament. In fact, they hardly even notice you. You wake up feeling extremely awkward. If you are fortunate, you may have had an interesting variation of this dream in which, perhaps after a series of embarrassing dreams of this nature, you find yourself once again on a toilet in a public setting but this time it doesn't bother you at all. As you take care of your business, you may even have friendly discussions with friends or people in the vicinity. You wake up surprised.

WHAT OTHERS HAVE SAID

In 200 C.E. Artemidorus wrote, "To defecate while one is sitting on a toilet . . . and to discharge a great amount of fecal matter means good luck for all men. For it signifies the alleviation of many cares and of all distress."[11] Many psychoanalysts have interpreted this dream as referring to the dreamer's pride of production as well as to shame, toilet training, and early sexual behavior. In my experience, the interpretation of this dream is usually much simpler and more direct. Let's take a look at a typical example.

SAMPLE DREAM

No Walls for the Bathroom

Josee dreamt: "I was in a small group of friendly people when I suddenly realized I had to go to the bathroom. The toilet was in the middle of the room and I was very embarrassed, but I was also very much in need and I wasn't quite sure what to do. Then I woke up."

Josee had just joined one of our dream study groups. We meet weekly, and each person in the group practices interviewing skills with the dreamer of the week. Many of the people had been in the group for over a year, and Josee was a new member. When one of the group members interviewed her, she asked, "Josee, why do humans have to go to the bathroom?" Josee answered, "To relieve themselves of waste products and get on with life! Okay! In the dream group, I have to show myself, even the embarrassing parts. You will all see me, and I'm a bit shy. But just like the spectators in the dream, you don't think it's a big deal at all."

WHAT DO YOU SAY?

1. Why do humans go to the bathroom?
2. What is uncomfortable about doing it in public?
3. How do you feel in the dream?
4. Is there a situation in your life in which you feel as you do in the dream and feel you have no privacy to do your business?
5. How so? Elaborate to see if this is a strong bridge.

Meeting a Friend You Haven't Seen in Years

VARIATIONS

Why in the world would you dream of Henry Vaccaro, whom you haven't seen since fifth grade? Or of Mrs. Gutterman, who was your high school science teacher? Or of your closest buddy from your senior year in college? Isn't it amazing how you can bring these people back to mind in a dream? When you wake up it is almost as if you really spent time with that person. Your old friend may have played the role of a dream companion or a dream ally, maybe even a dream enemy. Dreaming of people we haven't seen for years puzzles everyone, but it amuses us all.

WHAT OTHERS HAVE SAID

Interpretations of meeting a long-ago friend in a dream are limitless because the roles of your friends in the dream are limitless. Orthodox psychoanalysts might interpret an old friend of the same sex as an image of a sibling rivalry or a homosexual or lesbian interest. An old friend who is older than the dreamer might be interpreted as a mother or father image, and so on. Modern psychoanalysts, Jungians, and the more contemporary dream analysts would interpret the presence of this old friend according to the roles he or she played in the dreamer's life and the role cast for the character in the dream. In general, the old friend would be seen to represent certain qualities in the dreamer's personality and behavior or certain qualities in caricature form of someone important in the dreamer's current life, such as a boss, a mate, a sibling, or a friend. Because we remember people from our past in simpler terms than those in our present, we vividly highlight certain characteristics and traits or certain qualities of our relationship with them, and these we use to highlight certain qualities in ourselves or our current relationships.

SAMPLE DREAMS

With Sasha Again

Katya dreamt: "Sasha was moving into my apartment. We had apparently decided to live together, but I was feeling a little uncomfortable and not sure I wanted to do this."

I asked Katya to describe Sasha and tell me what sort of personality he had. She said, "Well, Sasha was a friend I haven't seen since high school. I liked him very much. He was a faithful friend and a very good student, responsible and dependable." I asked how she felt about him in the dream. She answered that it was nice to be with him because she liked him so much, but she was a bit concerned about his moving in because he was a little somber, a little too serious, and she thought it might be slightly oppressive

to have him living with her. I asked her if there were anyone in her current life who was like Sasha used to be when
she knew him—a good friend, dependable, a good student,
but a little too somber. She said, "Well, my current boyfriend is a little like that. I really admire him because he is
so dependable, so stable. I really like him, I love him, but
you know, he is a little bit like Sasha. A little bit too serious. And he wants to get more serious in our relationship.
I just couldn't stand it if he turns out to be a lot like Sasha;
it just wouldn't work."

Thugs Chase Us

Jeantul dreamt: "I was in a friendly bar with my old friend
Jacques. We were having a good time talking about life.
We went for a walk in what turned out to be a very bad
part of town. Some thugs were pursuing us, and I woke up
running away from them."

I asked Jeantul to describe Jacques, and he said he had
been a good friend when they were youths in France. He
hadn't seen him for a long time. I asked, "What is his personality like?" Jeantul said, "He was a good man, philo-
sophically oriented, but he drank too much, he was an
alcoholic, and I haven't seen him for at least a decade." I
asked Jeantul if there were anyone in his life or any part of
himself that was like Jacques: a good fellow, a philosophi-
cal one, and an alcoholic. Jeantul said no, so I looked for
other clues and asked, "What was it like to find yourself in
the bad part of town running from thugs?" He said it was
a surprise and that they were definitely in the wrong place
at the wrong time. He added, "I would normally know
better than to put myself in that part of town." I asked
him, "Is there any part of yourself or someone in your life

like Jacques with whom you sit around and talk about the meaning of the world and philosophize and drink and then get yourself into trouble, being in a place you know you shouldn't be, and having thugs threatening you?" At this point Jeantul said he had been drinking too much lately, if the truth were told, and he had been telling himself he was just going through a phase of self-reflection. Deep down he knew that he was playing with fire and that he was in the wrong part of his psychological town. He concluded, "By drinking too much several nights a week I know I've been putting myself in danger."

WHAT DO YOU SAY?

1. Describe your old friend from the dream as he or she was when you had regular contact with each other.

2. Describe how your friend was in the dream.

3. Is there anyone in your life who has the traits of this friend, which you describe as (restate the description)? Or is there any part of yourself that is like your friend?

4. How so? Elaborate on the parallels you see.

5. What is your friend doing in the dream?

6. What effect does your friend have upon you in the dream?

7. Is there any way that the action in the dream parallels a situation in your current life?

8. How so? Elaborate on the connection if you have found one.

9. Would you say that in the dream your friend plays the role of a friend, ally, or enemy? Does your friend play a positive role or a negative one?

10. During the next few days remember this friend and the role she or he played in your dream and see if you can identify these qualities or behaviors in your daily life.

Falling Dreams

VARIATIONS

Falling dreams are perhaps the most common dreams of all. Many of us have experienced a sense of suddenly falling on the ground or slipping on some ice just as we are falling asleep and our body begins to relax. We suddenly jerk, and the image in our mind is a quick scene of falling. These dreams usually do not interpret well. They seem not to be dreams at all, in fact, but quick images created as a response to relaxing and a quick jerk. These dreams are normal and usually don't have much to do with us on a psychological level.

However, we may have other falling dreams during the night that involve story lines and are normal dreams. In some we fall off a cliff or out of a plane. Sometimes someone trips us and we fall; other times we don't even know what precipitated the fall, we are just aware of falling, falling, falling. Most people are very frightened during their fall, and many worry that if they fall in a dream and hit the ground they will die and never wake up. I can reassure you that I have spoken to many dreamers who have fallen, hit the ground, and lived to tell about it. So, not to worry! Our falling dreams can carry important messages that express anxiety and dangerous, sometimes self-destructive behaviors.

WHAT OTHERS HAVE SAID

In the Talmud dreams of falling were considered to be an omen of dishonor. To fall into an abyss was to suggest a future danger. Freud, of course, had a predictable interpretation for falling dreams. He wrote, "Dreams of falling . . .

are more often characterized by anxiety. Their interpretation offers no difficulty in the case of women, who almost always accept the symbolic use of falling as a way of describing a surrender to an erotic temptation."[12] He also suggests that falling dreams may mean giving birth, and elsewhere he says, "If a woman dreams of falling it almost invariably has a sexual sense, she is imagining herself as a 'fallen woman.'"[13]

The Dreamland Companion author, Ilan Kutz,[14] notes, "Falling is sometimes related to the experience of having stumbled which was registered only by subliminal memory and surfaced for some reason in the dream." He and many other authors believe that falling dreams could also contain warnings about a potential literal fall such as a ladder or a step that has been in bad repair and has been ignored for too long and could potentially cause a fall. Both psychoanalysts and Jungians have interpreted some falling dreams as expressing a dreamer's fear of losing status, of being put down, or of feeling like a failure. Sometimes these dreams express a sense of lost control, of losing one's grip, and of being helpless and in an emotional free fall. Some people who have recurring blues or depressions will dream about falling and will interpret these dreams as signaling another recurrence of the depression.

SAMPLE DREAMS

Running, Falling

Bernard dreamt: "I was running along the edge of a cliff, running very fast because I felt I had to get to wherever I was going. I didn't notice a big rock in the path. I stumbled on it and fell into a huge and apparently endless abyss. I woke up just before I hit bottom, terrified."

In falling dreams we find it especially useful to discover what was going on just before the fall, what precipitated the fall, and how these two things relate to some situation in the dreamer's life. I asked Bernard to describe the action in the dream just before the fall. He said that he was running and felt very pressured to keep doing so. He knew he had to get somewhere on time, and he felt he was late. I asked him if these situations reminded him of anything in his life. He said yes, indeed, that's how he felt at work. Work was taking up most of his lifetime. I asked him if the rushing had anything to do with his tripping on the rock, and he said yes, that had he been taking his time he would have noticed the rock. But here he was running so fast he didn't see it and wasn't careful enough, therefore he lost his footing and fell. He interpreted the dream to be a warning about the emotional and health dangers he was running by being always stressed and always hurried. He worried that he would hurt his physical health or that at one point he would emotionally be incapable of keeping up the pace. He realized that not keeping up was a horrible thought because he was afraid that if he didn't keep running in his life, he would be worthless and would have no status and no wealth.

Trap Door Fall

Mary Lisa dreamt: "I was going over to my psychotherapist's office, and as I opened the door I stepped on a trap door and suddenly was falling down, down, down until I ended up in the sewers of Paris. I was very anxious and didn't know what I would find there. I awoke quite frightened."

Mary Lisa described a trap door as a kind of ambush carefully planned by another person to put the victim in a completely different place. She immediately bridged this to her feelings that her therapist in helping her try to understand the causes of her current difficulties in her relationships and at work was ambushing her and taking her into dark and unknown places in her life and in her psyche. She said the Paris sewers were useful places that kept the city functions flowing. She had never been in them and didn't know if one would find rats there or scary creatures or what. She said that was how she felt about exploring her deepest emotions. She was afraid that if she really let herself know what she was feeling, her feelings might be frightening or unpleasant or sad because for years she had been trying to avoid the unpleasantness of much of her childhood. While she understood that she had to look beneath the surface of her life, she decided that her dream expressed a sense of ambush and that she needed to discuss with her therapist a more consensual approach to uncovering her inner conflicts. She wanted to feel that she had a companion and guide in her travels rather than a therapist who would ambush her and take her, without her consent, into scary places.

WHAT DO YOU SAY?

1. What happens in your dream just before you fall? What leads up to or precipitates a fall in your dream?

2. How exactly do you feel as you are falling? Find two or three adjectives that describe your feeling.

3. Is there any situation in your life where you feel or fear feeling the way you do in your dream?

4. Is there any situation in your life that is like the scene that precedes the fall in your dream?

5. If so, can you see how the dream action preceding the fall describes potentially self-defeating or self-destructive behaviors in your current life?

Pleasant Flying Dreams

VARIATIONS

Whenever I talk about dreams in a lecture or to a live audience in a television show, all I have to do is mention flying dreams and I hear a delighted "Ahhh!" ripple through the audience. I see smiles on many faces because flying dreams are among the most pleasant, delightful, and thrilling life experiences a human being can have. If you have had pleasant flying dreams, you know how wonderful it is to remember the delight, the thrill of soaring, the pleasure of flying effortlessly through the air, doing acrobatic stunts, flying high, flying low, seeing beautiful sights, and feeling unbelievably free.

If you haven't had a dream like this, you are very likely to have one once you recall your dreams more fully. In some people's flying dreams it is nighttime. I have flown over the San Francisco Bay and out on the West Coast over the cliffs and the ocean in the moonlight and under the stars. Others fly in daytime and see bright sun and beautiful mountaintops. Some people fly to friends' houses and visit. Some just float in their bedrooms and seem to be able to pass through walls and in and out of closed windows. Many people say that their earliest remembered flying dreams were pseudoflying dreams in which they might be swimming or skiing and say, "Ahhh! I think I'm flying." I had my earliest flying dreams of swimming and flying but also of ice skating. In these dreams I would take off for a jump in the air and find that I could use gravity at my will. I had to learn how not to over-jump out of the skating rink into the bleachers and how not to hit my head on the rafters above. It was quite a delightful challenge.

Many people have particular techniques for initiating flight in a dream. Early in people's dream-flying careers, dreamers usually expend a lot of effort getting airborne. People flap their arms really hard, as if they were wings; some people use a bent right leg as a rudder, others take a one, two, three jump, à la Superman, to get into the air, and still others spin in order to take off, sort of like a helicopter. What is amusing to note is that, as time goes on, dreamers become aware that they really don't have to go through all this fuss to take flight. Just the slight movement of a finger will do it and then later on dreamers say that actually all they need is the right attitude to get into the air. They have to know that they can fly and not worry about it, not doubt themselves, and just take off and everything works out fine.

WHAT OTHERS HAVE SAID

Throughout the ages no dreamer has been able to resist the temptation to explain flying dreams. In 200 C.E. Artemidorus had much to say about flying dreams: "If a man dreams that he is flying not very far above the earth and in an upright position it means good luck for the dreamer, the greater the distance above the earth, the higher his position will be in regard to those who walk beneath him for we always call those who are more prosperous the higher ones. . . ."

He goes on to write that "Flying with wings is auspicious for all men alike, the dream signifies freedom for slaves, since all birds that fly are without a master and have no one above them, it means that the poor will acquire a great deal of money, for just as money raises men up, wings raise birds up. It signifies offices for the rich and very influential, for just as the creatures of the air are above those that crawl upon the earth rulers are above private citizens. . . ."

He also added that "Flying with the birds signifies that one will dwell with men of far nationalities and with strangers. The dream is inauspicious for criminals since it signifies punishment for wrong doers and frequently even crucifixion."[15]

While Freud originally wrote that flying dreams always meant the same thing, he later wrote that such dreams "mean something different in every instance." Freud believed that these dreams were triggered by childhood memories of games of movement such as playing on seesaws and swings and being tossed in the air by adults, and he noted that although these games were innocent themselves, they often gave rise to sexual feelings. Then because Freud was aware that both the German and the Italian language use the word *bird* as a nickname for *penis,* Freud thought that flying dreams usually have "a grossly sensual meaning" and were often accompanied by erections and sometimes orgasms in men. He often called them dreams of erection. You may wonder what he said about the flying dreams of women: never at a loss for interpretation, Freud wrote that these dreams reflect the conscious or unconscious wish to be a man.

Many modern psychoanalysts recognize that flying dreams can be related to a far greater variety of human experiences. For example, Grinstein cautions that the dreamer's personal experiences of aviation, such as difficult flights, or of having read books that refer metaphorically to flying, where the word *flying* is associated with getting free of inhibitions or soaring with a greater sense of individuality and dedication to causes, will lead to very different and specific interpretations for a given dreamer at a given time in his or her life. Friedrich Nietzsche in his book *Beyond Good and Evil* wrote a wonderful description of the magic of flying dreams: "Suppose someone has flown often in his dreams and finally, as soon as he dreams, he is conscious of his power and art of flight as if it were his privilege, also his characteristic and enviable happiness. He believes himself capable of every kind of arc simply with the lightest impulse; he knows the feeling of a certain divine frivolity, an 'upward' without tension and constraint, a 'downward' without condescension and humiliation—without *gravity!* How could a human being who had had such dream experiences and dream habits fail to find that the word 'happiness' had a different color and definition in his waking life, too? How could he fail to desire happiness differently? 'Rising' as described by poets must seem to him, compared with this 'flying,' too earthbound, muscle-bound, forced, too 'grave.'"[16]

I encourage my clients to enjoy their pleasant flying dreams, to really savor the feeling of liberty or transcendence or whatever they feel. It is useful to ask oneself, "Why did I have the dream on this particular night? What happened yesterday? What has been going on in my life recently that would give rise to such a dream? Am I making a breakthrough, or am I telling myself that I really need to get free, I really need to get unstuffed to soar and fly?"

A common version of this dream is one in which the dreamer takes off and flies with the intent of showing everyone else that only she can fly, that she feels really above and superior to everyone else and loves showing off. Others dream of teaching people how to fly either by teaching them difficult movement—arm-flapping techniques, for example—or by talking to them about state of mind and showing them how to feel in order to be able to fly. The different ways you fly, your different concerns, your different activities with flight, and how you feel about those will all determine what your dream means to you. Let's take a look at a couple of my clients' dreams.

SAMPLE DREAMS

I Fly

Marilyn regularly has this dream: "I am flying above my colleagues and my friends, and I am the only one who can fly. They all marvel at my ability, and I am very proud of it."

When I interviewed Marilyn about this dream I didn't suggest an interpretation by saying that she wanted to be a man or that she was proud of her sexual prowess or that she wanted to be free or transcendent. Instead I asked her, "How do you feel in the dream?" She responded that she felt very happy to be able to do this in front of her friends and show them that she had an ability no one else had. I asked her if there was any way in her waking life that she does the same thing. She said, "Actually, in my career and maybe also with my social friends, I do show off and try to show myself as more spiritual than they are." As she spoke she realized that this may not be one of her more endearing qualities and that perhaps her need to be superior in the eyes of her friends was a compensation for feelings of inferiority, a compensation that could be rather distasteful to those around her.

Flying with Churchill

Frank dreamt that he had a chance to fly in the company of Winston Churchill. He was very excited, and he was trying to show Winston how able he was to complete complicated acrobatic feats in the air. He was having lots of fun and enjoying showing his prowess to Winston. Now and then he worried that he might not be able to keep his altitude, but he knew that if he worried for an instant he would lose his altitude. So he just kept his mind focused on the pleasure of showing off his skills.

Frank described Winston Churchill as a man who had the enormous courage to say what needed to be said, a man who knew how to encourage vast numbers of people, and a man whose ability to thrive under enormous pressure was legend. When I asked him to describe what his flying felt like, he said he was simply and enormously pleased that the time had come in his life when he could finally do this. "I'm at a level of achievement in my life where I feel really competent. I didn't feel obnoxious; I felt proud, and Winston was happy to see me, as if he were encouraging me to join the ranks of men who performed extraordinarily well." The dream concerned Frank's growing sense of himself as a mature man of great achievement and skill.

WHAT DO YOU SAY?

1. What is it like when you fly? Do you have any trouble getting or maintaining your altitude? Are there any other obstacles, concerns, or happenings in the dream?
2. How do you feel while flying in your dream?
3. Tell me more about these feelings.

4. What, if any, are the obstacles (include attitudes, doubts, and so forth) to your flying or to your feeling great about flying in your dream?

5. Do the obstacles in your dream remind you of any obstacles in your waking life?

6. When was the last time you felt in waking life the way you do in the dream?

7. So, does your flying, which feels (restate the description), remind you of any situation in your life? Does it remind you of any feelings you wish you felt in your life?

Unpleasant Flying Dreams

VARIATIONS

Even flying dreams can be spoiled by anxiety and hostility and insecurity. Commonly, people dream of trying to fly and of not being able to get off the ground. Or they may finally, after a lot of arm flapping and struggling, get into the air only to worry about losing altitude or about bumping into things or about getting tangled up with high tension wires. Others have trouble getting out of an enclosed space; they want to fly but can't get through the window or the ceiling and feel stuck. Sometimes the dreamer is trying to fly, trying to take off, but is unable to because someone is holding onto his or her foot and won't let the person go. Such dreams can be filled with frustration and anxiety. Another common version of this dream is one in which the dreamer is running away from a pursuer, a bad guy or an animal, and in running, the dreamer can take off and start to fly. In this case the flight is used as escape from fear and anxiety.

WHAT OTHERS HAVE SAID

In the second century C.E. Artemidorus interpreted a dream of flying while one is "being pursued by a wild animal, a man or a demon to portend great fears and dangers."[17] He interpreted dreams in which one wants to fly but is unable to as foretelling much misfortune to the dreamer. Traditional psychoanalytic interpretations about dreams in which the dreamer can't get off the ground or the dreamer fears altitude focus on fear of loss of an erection or sexual prowess. At our dream center we (along with most modern psychotherapists) have found problems in flying dreams to have far more varied meanings. Men and women who fear losing their altitude often are afraid of losing their sense of well-being or of losing their ability to feel free and to soar emotionally, and some even have the fear of losing their financial security. When people dream of flying in order to escape difficult situations, demons, or wild animals, it is often useful to ask the dreamer if that is his or her current way of coping with difficult situations. Does the dreamer often try to escape, to get above it all rather than deal effectively with the situation? When obstacles stand in the way of the flight or people try to hold the dreamer down, the meaning of the dream depends entirely upon the dreamer's description of the obstructing things or people. I have also seen a flying dream in which the dreamer was unable to get through a certain ceiling in the room because a netting prevented her from flying away; this dream reflected the dreamer's effort to break a marijuana habit, where getting high had caused her a lot of problems in her relationship to her infant child.

SAMPLE DREAMS

He Won't Let Me Fly

Carol dreamt she was in her backyard trying to take off for flight, but she couldn't get any higher than about six feet. She kept flapping her wings or her arms, until finally she looked down and saw that her husband was holding onto her ankle and wouldn't let her go.

When I asked her to describe her husband and how he was acting in the dream, she said he was a loving man but one who was extremely possessive and who could not stand the idea that she should start a career. He had been resisting her going to night school for that reason. "I feel like he is holding me down, and I feel very frustrated in my waking life, just as I do in the dream."

Bailing Out

Hasse dreamt: "I was flying in an airplane, and I thought the airplane was going to crash, so I pushed the eject button and I bailed out."

I interviewed Hasse, asking him how it felt knowing that the plane was likely to crash. He said it was very uncomfortable; he didn't want to go down with the plane so he bailed out.

I asked if there was any current situation in his life that feels like he is on a flight that is going to crash, where the plane is going down and he doesn't want to go down with it so he decides to bail out. He said, "Yes, I've decided to leave my alcoholic wife and I am bailing out. I can't save this marriage, and I'm not going to go down with the plane. I really do have to leave and it's very difficult, but the situation is dire."

WHAT DO YOU SAY?

See "Pleasant Flying Dreams" for the basic interview questions. Here are some additional questions for unpleasant flying dreams:

1. Describe the person or obstacle that is inhibiting your flight.
2. Describe the feeling or insecurity that is inhibiting your flight.
3. Is there anything or anyone in your life that is like the thing in the dream that is causing you trouble?
4. Describe how you use flight in the dream (to escape, to show off, and so forth).
5. Does the way you use flight in your dream parallel ways you have of coping with pleasant or threatening situations in your waking life?

Missing the Plane, Train, Boat, or Bus

VARIATIONS

The dream of missing the plane or boat or bus has many variations, most of them resulting in very frustrated feelings for the dreamer. Do you remember missing a bus because you hadn't packed your clothing in time or not being able to get on the bus because you had so much luggage you couldn't fit through the front door? Perhaps you've dreamt that you missed a flight that you had forgotten all about or that you had taken too long in traffic to get to the airport and so missed the plane. Some people get distracted along the way to their vehicles and miss the boat because something else was going on and the dreamer lost track of time. Some people get to the boat or the train and find that they forgot their tickets or that they are there on the wrong day; the train took off yesterday. Often in these dreams there's a terrible feeling of rushing against insurmountable odds, and usually the dreamer is quite disappointed to have missed the boat.

WHAT OTHERS HAVE SAID

Because Freud thought it was self-evident that dreams of departing or going on a journey were symbols of death, he interpreted dreams of missing a train or a bus as dreams of consolation. These dreams, he thought, are saying, Don't worry, you are not going to die; you missed the bugle call that was going to take you on the trip to the other side. Given this presupposition, some psychoanalysts also believe that these dreams can be suggestive of suicidal thought in the dreamer, where the dreamer is seen to be expressing feelings and thoughts of hopelessness and despair by trying to take off on a trip. Psychoanalysts often think that the anxieties associated with these dreams refer to castration, loss, abandonment, and rejection.

Alexander Grinstein writes that missing a train may have to do with a play on the word *train,* referring to the individual's training, education, and sexual enlightenment, but more specifically to toilet training. In this case missing the train may refer to times in which the dreamer lacked sphincter control or had an accident, and he suggests that the cars of the train in such instances could refer to feces in such a dream, suggesting the dreamer's fear of having an accident. I have never seen these interpretations flow from the descriptions of a dream interview, although the abandonment hypothesis seems a plausible one.

When I ask dreamers to tell me how they feel about missing the boat or the plane and to describe what led up to that situation, I see interpretations dealing with a feeling of lost opportunity, a feeling of fear and anxiety that holds one back from whatever one must do, or a feeling of frustration and sometimes guilt at not having lived up to an obligation or a felt duty in the world. Some people have this type of dream frequently, and in interviews with them we often discover that they have such overscheduled lives with so many deadlines and so much pressure that they regularly feel they are missing a deadline or an opportunity to live a happier life. Again, everything depends upon the specifics of the dream and on the dreamer's feelings about both the images in the dream and the context of his or her life. Dreamers who suddenly discover they have forgotten a trip entirely usually can bridge these experiences to some project in life or some project at work of which they have lost track. Dreams in which the dreamer is distracted by other people, other events, and or rather unimportant activities usually have something to do with the dreamer's procrastination with making an important step in her psychological growth or in the actual structure of her life or relationships or career.

SAMPLE DREAMS

Missing the Plane

Jenna, during the course of a two-year-long study group, collected a long series of flying dreams with very interesting results. In her dreams Jenna kept missing the plane because she had forgotten to pack her luggage or forgotten her tickets. Or a bird was unable to fly because of fear and inability. Or she waited too long and missed her flight. Or once, given a free airline ticket and rushing to catch the plane, she was unable to find the airport and missed the flight. All of these circumstances seemed to her to represent missed opportunities to live a fuller, more exciting, freer life. During that period she was in a very unhappy relationship with a man, and it wasn't until she had learned enough about herself and the dynamics of the relationship, with a great deal of help from her dream work, that she was able both to leave the relationship and to dream of actually flying. Her dreams reflected her new ability to soar and her new sense of her own power.

Rush for the Orient Express

Cici dreamt: "I was getting ready to take the Orient Express, a wonderful train ride through an exotic part of Europe, and I was packing my bags. I thought I had another three hours and had plenty of time to get to the station when suddenly I looked at my watch and I only had five minutes. Where had the time gone? Had my watch been wrong? I rushed like mad, and the dream ends where I'm still rushing to the station and know that it is too late, I'm not going to make it."

When Cici described her feelings and the action in the dream she said, "Thinking I had plenty of time reminds me of having told my best girlfriend yesterday that I had plenty of time to find a man, get married, and have a family. This dream reminds me that I have been fooling myself. I'm already thirty-six, and if I don't put my mind to it I'll be too old to have babies comfortably. For me, going on the Orient Express is a great adventure, and that's how I feel marriage and having children would be."

WHAT DO YOU SAY?

1. How do you feel about missing your plane, train, boat, or bus?

2. Do you know why in the dream you are missing your boat (or bus or train or plane)?

3. Do you see any parallels between the cause of your missing the dream vehicle and any attitudes, behaviors, or circumstances in your life?

4. Does whatever causes you to miss the boat in the dream also cause you to miss the boat in life?

5. Do you have trouble getting where you want to go in life because you are always too rushed, unprepared, or distracted or overburdened, etc.?

6. What might you be able to do to remedy the situation?

PART 2

Dream Elements

2 People in Dreams

How to Interpret Any Person in Your Dreams

Since no book or even computer software could ever list the cast of thousands who have appeared in your dreams, you will find it helpful to keep in mind the following Dream Interview questions, which you can ask yourself or a friend about any person who appears in the sagas of your nights.

1. Who is this person? Pretend I've never heard of him or her before.

2. What is this person like in waking life? Describe with three or four adjectives.

3. What is this person like in your dream, and what is he or she up to?

4. Do you like this person or not? Elaborate.

5. So you describe this person as (restate the description), right?

6. Does this person, whom you describe as (restate the description), remind you of anything or anyone in your life?

7. Does this person remind you of any part of yourself?

8. How so? Test the bridge, or connection, to your waking life by elaborating on how the dream image fits the waking one. See if this is a good metaphorical match. If not, get a more complete description of the person to see if you can clarify the connection.

You may add to this list questions specific to your particular dream, and you may not need to ask all these questions; sometimes one or two questions will bring forth the meaning of the dream. Keep in mind that your imagined dream interviewer pretends to have come from another planet and knows nothing about the people, even the very famous people, in your dreams. Imagining this will encourage you to give concise, honest descriptions of what you like and don't like about the person and his or her behavior in your dream. After you have described the dream person and after you have asked if this description reminds you of anyone you know or of any part of yourself or of any situation in your life, you should be able to arrive, with practice, at a tailor-made interpretation that makes sense to you and that helps you understand yourself and your life better.

Movie and TV Stars

VARIATIONS

Most people are usually thrilled to dream about movie and TV stars. Usually, but not always, the dreamer feels flattered by attention from someone who is seen as glamorous and exciting. Sometimes the stars act out of character. Sometimes they appear in your dreams as the character they play on the screen, and sometimes they appear as the actor in his or her private life. There is no limit to the roles these famous people can play or to the meanings they can carry for you. You might make love to your favorite movie star and feel greatly flattered, or you may be told that you are not welcome at a party given by your favorite screen actor. Then again, your favorite actors or characters may be in dire straits and in need of your help in a dream.

WHAT OTHERS HAVE SAID

Famous people in dreams have been interpreted in a myriad of ways. Psychoanalysts tend to see a father image in older male characters, a mother image in older female characters, and so forth. At the Delaney & Flowers Dream Center we elicit a rich, definitive description of the character before we begin to hypothesize what meaning he or she may have for the dreamer. Let's take a look at a few examples.

SAMPLE DREAMS

Jerry Seinfeld and George

Linda dreamt: "I need to go to school and register for classes. I have a pressing urgency to get to school. I'm registering late as it is. I have a transportation problem, and I get the idea that I will go to Jerry Seinfeld's apartment and then use George's car. George has a somewhat faded red Volkswagen. I do get to school on time."

Linda described Jerry Seinfeld as a funny, cynical, and disparaging man whose humor was always a put-down. She bridged that description to her life by seeing that it fit none other than her husband. She described George as Seinfeld's sidekick, a person who was always around, who was also cynical, and who was not the main star. She bridged George to herself, saying, "My husband has the primary position in our business, and I feel like the sidekick and his assistant." Linda then described George's faded red Volkswagen as a car with an engine in the back, no trunk, no room for storage, and no place to carry anything extra, a car whose red lifeblood was faded from being outside and not having its own garage. She said, "My body, my self, is like George's car. My role in the company is not primary, and I feel that I really do need to start school and start a career of my own. I think that while I am attracted to Jerry Seinfeld, I really need not to play George to him; I need to have my own career that is separate, where I feel that I am the primary mover rather than the assistant."

Faye Dunaway

Anna dreamt: "I am trying to save a wonderful woman from being executed. She is like Faye Dunaway in *Don Juan de Marco*, a current movie. I am pleading for her, but people won't listen or change their minds. They think she is different, strange, maybe bad, and therefore she must be killed. Suddenly someone says to me, 'It's too late, she's already dead.' I am so upset that I wake up crying."

Anna said that Faye Dunaway in her dream was the character she played in the movie *Don Juan de Marco*, so I asked her, "What is Faye Dunaway like in your dream?" She described her as an older woman, romantic and beautiful. Anna really liked her role because it reminded her of how she wanted to feel but how she did not feel in her current marriage. When I asked her what was happening to Faye in the dream, she said that Faye was going to be executed for no fault of her own. "She is just being different; that's really all it is. They call her bad, but she isn't. She's a being of romance and beauty, and it's terrible that they are going to kill her. Do you think the fact that in the dream she is already dead means it's too late for me? That that part of myself is dead and will never live again?" I reassured Anna that dreams often exaggerate to get their point across, and I returned the question to her, saying, "Do you think the Faye Dunaway in you is dead?" She said, "Oh, no, I still feel it, but I am afraid that if I act on it I will want to leave my husband and I will be terribly criticized by his family and perhaps by everyone." She knew she would have a difficult time earning a living, and that's why she had been putting off the decision for so long. "But this dream makes me think that I really must act, because I don't want to live the rest of my life without feeling what Faye Dunaway felt in the movie: romance, beauty, and happiness with a man she loved."

WHAT DO YOU SAY?

1. Is the star in your dream acting as himself or herself off-screen, or is the star staying in the role as a character you are familiar with on-screen?

2. What is the actor or screen character like in your dream?

3. How do you like this star? Why?

4. What is the star doing in your dream, and how do you feel about this?

5. Does this star, whom you describe as (restate the description), remind you of yourself or of anyone else in your life?

6. How so?

7. If the star does not remind you of anyone in your life or of a part of yourself, and if the main feeling in the dream is that you were incredibly flattered to get the star's attention, have you been needing a boost to your self-esteem lately?

Strangers

VARIATIONS

Strangers in our dreams are usually unsettling, puzzling, or threatening characters. Although we may not know the identity of the person, we usually know what the person looks like, how he or she is dressed, and how he or she acts in the dream. All these things are clues to the dream's meaning. Also, we usually know much more about a stranger in a dream than we at first suspect. Often we know what the stranger is feeling and what he or she intends. We almost always know how we feel in relation to that stranger and in reaction to his or her behavior. Suppose, for example, that you dream of a stranger at a party who is barefoot, dressed apparently only in a raincoat, and hiding in a corner. What do you think that stranger might be up to? What do you think his personality might be like? If you created the dream image, you usually have enough information to interpret it. We assign strangers innumerable roles in our dreams, from burglars to fairy godmothers to strangers at a dinner table to named or unnamed companions to benevolent, wise advice-givers whom we meet in a cave or in passing on a street corner.

WHAT OTHERS HAVE SAID

Karen Signell, a Jungian analyst, writes that a "burglar breaking into your house or a stranger chasing you may mean that some new element in your psyche is trying to break into consciousness, trying to reach you and be acknowledged."[1] Some traditional psychoanalysts interpret strangers and burglars as representing sexual intercourse or a sexual breaking in, such as a female dreamer's wish to be penetrated or as a male dreamer's homosexual wish for penetration. Some Jungians tend to emphasize the positive nature of the stranger or the burglars and ask questions such as, "What is the dreamer trying to keep out of her life? What part of herself or what characteristics is she defending against letting into her conscious awareness?" Dream dictionaries usually provide arbitrary interpretations of strangers appearing in dreams. For instance, one dictionary says that an unknown person, especially a brunette, "presages or foretells success in business; for a man [she] can represent his future wife."[2]

Almost all modern dream analysts would agree that strangers may represent an aspect of the dreamer's personality that is not yet well known or understood by the dreamer. They may also represent other people or forces in the dreamer's life, and they may represent institutions or personified fears. I have found that the specific interpretation depends upon the role the stranger plays in the dream, on the qualities the stranger expresses in his or her action or appearance, and on the feelings the dreamer has regarding the stranger.

Sometimes the stranger represents a force, an attitude, or a quality that the dreamer would do well to keep out of her life—not out of her awareness, but out of her life. By describing the nature of the burglar or the stranger, you can determine whether it is better to develop or reject these traits or qualities. For example, the wife who dreamt a thief was stealing her husband's favorite food from the refrigerator understood her dream to be about the destructive affair she was having, which siphoned off her most erotic energies and thereby threatened her marriage.

SAMPLE DREAMS

How Can I Help the Little Girl?

Cristal dreamt: "I was in a grocery store, and I saw a mother mercilessly criticizing her little daughter, who had only touched a package of candy on a display counter." Cristal felt terrible for the little girl and found the mother to be verbally abusive but couldn't find the words to protect the little girl.

Cristal described the little girl as being quiet, well behaved but a little timid, and about five years old. I asked her if this reminded her of any part of herself or anyone in her life, and she said she didn't know. So we went on to the next image, and I asked her to describe the mother. Cristal said the mother was overly strict and didn't realize she was being abusive and was breaking the spirit of the little girl by shaming her in public. When I asked Cristal if this stranger, the mother in the dream, reminded her of anyone in her life, she said she reminded her of her own mother and the little girl reminded her of her own feelings in the face of her mother's criticism and excessive efforts to control her. I asked Cristal why she might be having this dream just now. She responded that her mother had been dead for years but that perhaps she was still living as if her mother were alive inside her head, criticizing her and telling her not to reach out for things. Cristal said she goes through much of life fearing a critical attack by others just as she feared it when she was a girl.

Burglars

I once dreamt of burglars who used screwdrivers to pry open the sliding door of my home. I later discovered they had stolen all my favorite music and favorite jewelry, which had been romantic gifts from my husband and former boyfriends. In trying to chase down the burglars, I found them pinning a mother against a wall, totally immobilizing her.

When I interviewed myself about the dream, describing the burglars and their actions, I realized that the way the burglars had gained entrance to the home was how I pictured a sperm getting around a diaphragm. The burglars immobilizing the mother brought to mind my disinclination to have children because as a mother I felt I would be pinned against a wall and would have much more difficulty finding time for my career and my other passionate interests in life. The burglars' stealing the most romantic things in my life underlined my concern that having children would take much of the romance out of my life, as I had seen it do in the marriages of so many friends. These strangers, the burglars, represented to me the idea of having children and how it would rob from me the things I valued most in my life.

WHAT DO YOU SAY?

Here are interview questions that will help you understand why you dream of strangers.

1. Describe the stranger in your dream. What is his personality like? What is her intent?

2. What else can you say about the stranger given his or her dress and behavior?

3. How do you feel about the stranger and his or her behavior in the dream?

4. Is there anywhere in your life where you feel the way you do in the dream?

5. Is there anyone in your life, any part of yourself, or anything in your life that is like the stranger, whom you describe as (restate the description)?

6. How so? Be as specific as you can.

Royalty and Politicians

VARIATIONS

How many dreams do you think Princess Diana has starred in over the last ten years? People love to dream about royalty and politicians. Winston Churchill, Prince Charles, the Queen Mother, and our presidents make regular appearances in the dreams of Americans. People who are interested in royalty and politicians of different countries and different periods of time use their images to represent aspects of themselves and the people, hopes, and goals in their lives. Margaret Thatcher was popular during the Reagan administration, as Princess Grace of Monaco was popular twenty years ago. Politicians and royalty capture our imaginations and crystallize for us, often in caricature form, certain traits or ways of being that are important to us. Images of Idi Amin or Stalin may cause us no end of trouble in our dreams, while more positively viewed characters are likely to help us out. Young romantics dream of being courted by princes or princesses.

The remarkable vividness and clarity of some of these dreams is often a special treat. Where else can you dance with Bill Clinton, dine with Clayton Powell, or ride up the Thames with Prince Charles? It is interesting to note that as the public image of a particular character changes, so also does the meaning this character holds for the dreamer. Whereas around the time of his wedding Prince Charles was often dreamt of in glowing romantic terms, he now is often pictured in dreams as the cold and faithless husband who wanted a wife simply for formal and dynastic reasons but who withheld his love. Of course, others who hold the prince in highest esteem might dream of him as a person who has the courage to speak out for what he believes in, as Charles has been known to do regarding unpopular issues in his home country. The meaning of a royal person or politician depends upon the dreamer's perceptions of that person and on the particular aspects of personality that the dreamer happens to be most interested in.

WHAT OTHERS HAVE SAID

The psychoanalyst Alexander Grinstein notes that queens and important female social political figures can represent the dreamer's mother. Jung offered fascinating and complicated formulations for the meaning of kings and queens, who may represent the core self of the dreamer. The king may represent the concept of logos, the word or the thinking function; the queen may represent the feeling function of the dreamer. Regents might represent the wise old man or the wise old woman believed to be an archetype of wisdom in each of us. Princesses and princes can lead the dreamer into deeper levels of the self or may be simple representations of the dreamer as the child of the more powerful parent. Psychoanalysts James Fosshage and Clemens Loew write, "Persons endowed with authority symbolize the parents."[3] Kings and queens and presidents and governors can be apt representations of family, friends, and lovers. They can also represent deep psychological forces in the dreamer's self. Or they may represent employers, church leaders, or others in positions of authority in the dreamer's life.

SAMPLE DREAM

Marry Prince Charles?

Iris dreamt: "Prince Charles asked me to marry him. I was thrilled, but then I suddenly remembered the terrible tales of the power and control exerted by his family. I worried that I, like Diana, would be held prisoner in a rigid, loveless castle and would never have any real intimacy with my husband, the prince."

Iris described Prince Charles as a man who did not have control over his own life and who married for reasons of form, not of love. She realized the man she was presently engaged to shared many of these characteristics. Worst of all, she had to admit that her fiancé's family thought themselves superior to her and her family and were well known in the community for being extraordinarily controlling and rigid people. Her dream helped Iris reconsider her marriage choice.

WHAT DO YOU SAY?

1. What role does the politician or royal person play in your dream?

2. Describe this person's personality. Since you may not know him or her personally, describe the personality as you think it is. Remember to describe this individual as if you were speaking to someone who comes from another planet.

3. What is this person like in your dream? What part of this person's role or personality is being highlighted?

4. How do you like this person in general and in your dream? Explain why you do or do not like the person.

5. Does this person, who is (recap the personality description) and who plays the role of (restate the description), remind you of a person or of a quality of yourself or of someone close to you?

6. How so? Be specific and make sure you have a good match.

Mafia, Nazis, Fascists, and Dictators

VARIATIONS

Powerful men who are interested in total control and who will do anything to get what they want often show up in dreams of mobsters, fascists, and dictators. They may be Mafia men who kidnap the dreamer or who impersonate businessmen and friends, Nazis who threaten execution if you don't do what they want, fascists who export Jews to the Nazis, or ruthless dictators who threaten the dreamer or other people in the dream scene. Sometimes non-Jewish dreamers will dream of being sent off to concentration camps or of trying to liberate Jews who are being murdered by the Nazis. I have even heard dreams of dictators trying to mend their ways and explaining to the dreamer that they had turned into ruthless despots because of early childhood feelings of inferiority that now they were beginning to overcome.

WHAT OTHERS HAVE SAID

Many psychoanalysts treat despotic male dream characters as father images. Many Jungians see them as archetypal representations of the shadow or disowned part of the dreamer or as images of negative male aspects of female dreamers. Existentialists tend to see them as expressing ways of feeling and being of which the dreamer becomes aware in the dream.

At our dream center, many dreamers have told us that Mafia men represent caricatures of people in their lives who will stop at nothing to get what they want. Nazis, fascists, and dictators are also described similarly, although Nazis are often seen as the most repressive, controlling, hateful people, sometimes reminding dreamers of their parents or of dreamers' own rigid, repressive personality traits. Dictators may represent a part of the dreamer's own personality that is very dictatorial and rigid, or the dreamer may use such images to represent parents, employers, or spouses.

Frequently the overcontrolling rigid fascist or dictator is used as an image by women to represent their feelings of being controlled or of being powerless in a relationship with a man.

SAMPLE DREAMS

The Mafia Is Going to Kill Me

Mimi dreamt: "Because of my attachment to a Mafia man, I am to be killed by his henchman. At one point I expect to be strafed by planes overhead, and I try to prepare myself for the inevitable. I awake in the middle of the night, terrified."

Mimi had gone to sleep asking herself if the man she loved was indeed a con man, as all her friends thought. In describing a Mafia man, Mimi said, "They are 100 percent self-centered; they think of themselves first no matter what they say to the contrary, and they have no scruples about taking advantage of other people, even to the point of killing them for personal gain." Since the dream opened with the declaration that her attachment to a Mafia man was the cause of her impending death, she added, "Well, the only man I'm attached to right now is Michael, and my friends all think he's a con man. They have lots of reasons to think that he is. I have lots of reasons to think that he loves me and is just going through a difficult time in his life. But my friends may be right." Mimi described a henchman as someone who does the dirty work for the Mafia, the power man. She thought that the henchman was the part of her boyfriend who was used to taking advantage of women, even if there was another part of him that was loving and kind. She thought that perhaps the henchman would win out, and she knew that she could be financially ruined by this man. The dream was a wake-up call.

Fleeing Il Duce

Francesca dreamt: "At a 1930s-type European stadium, a man like Mussolini, Il Duce, has some apartments up on the right. The man is scruffy and has lots of power. He wants me. I am trying to get away, smiling. At another time I remember I had been with a blond guy, same story. . . . He was up on the left, he wanted me. I got away by smiling. He was less offensive but underneath had the same problem: wanting to control me, to possess me. I plan to get out of the country with a dark-haired mousy woman later that evening. A streetwise friend comes up to me to give me survival advice: 'I wouldn't leave with that woman. You'll never make it. Just get out now.'"

Francesca described Il Duce as the best-dressed, hippest dictator the world has ever known, a fascist who wanted to make himself look important by controlling others. Il

Duce in her dream was focused primarily on power and wanted her in a heartless and acquisitive manner. She said that certain aspects of Il Duce reminded her of her current boyfriend, although she thought he was certainly not a heartless man. Yet the second, blond, dictator in the dream reminded her very much of her former husband, who underneath his more agreeable facade was extremely controlling and unwilling or unable to let her live her own life. She said that she had recently been trying to withdraw from her lover because she had felt overly controlled by him. She was trying to do it in a nice manner, very gently and in a smiling way. Looking at her dream, she feared that she would be unable to exit this relationship gracefully, but she still resisted her dream friend's streetwise advice that she should just get out abruptly and completely while she was still able. As it turned out, she postponed breaking up with her boyfriend for another three months, only to find that it was more difficult to break up because she had become more and more entwined and he had become more and more dependent upon her.

Family Members

VARIATIONS

So many of our dreams are peopled by those we grew up with or are currently living with that it's hard to imagine a dream in which family members could not make an appearance. The things to look out for are the following: What roles do your family members play? Are these roles positive or negative? Are they helping or hindering you?

How frequently do particular family members recur in your dreams?

In some dreams we want to kill someone in our family; in others we grieve over a dream death that has not occurred in waking reality. Sometimes we tell off our parents or mate in ways we never had the courage to do while awake. Sometimes we discover new depths of tender and loving feelings for a brother or an aunt to whom we are not very close in waking life. These dreams can be terrifying when a family member tries to do us great harm in a dream. Dreams of physical or sexual abuse by family members are important warning signs of serious trouble either in that particular relationship or in one that is similar to it. If you have dreams like this, I encourage you to read chapter 8 of my book *Sensual Dreaming* and to consider consulting a psychotherapist for at least a few sessions to see where such painful images come from in your life. These dreams do not necessarily mean that you have been sexually abused; they do, however, express deep pain and a sense of helplessness in that relationship. Left untended, these feelings could lead you to repeat similar relationships in your adult life, which would bring you only more pain and suffering.

WHAT OTHERS HAVE SAID

Gestalt therapists tend to follow the rigid dictum that every image in your dream represents a part of the dreamer. Thus any family member in your dream would be a caricature or representation of aspects of your personality or feelings that you have projected upon the image of the family member. While almost all contemporary analysts agree that sometimes your family members represent parts of your own personality, this is not generally accepted for many, and perhaps the majority of, such dreams. For example, consider the dream of a woman who has been sexually abused and dreams of being sexually abused by her father. To ask her to interpret her father as her own aggressiveness would be ludicrous. Carl Jung had this rule of thumb: when we dream of people with whom we are not in regular contact, these people tend to represent some aspect of the dreamer's personality or someone in the dreamer's life who is like the dream figure. However, when we dream about people with whom we have regular contact, it is likely such images represent some aspect of the person pictured in the dream image. Thus the woman dreaming of her abusive father is dreaming about her relationship to this man. This dream might also come at a time in her adult life in which she is currently involved in another abusive relationship. The dream then can serve to express similar feelings triggered in the current but repetitive situation.

At our dream center we ask people first to describe the person in the dream (see the first entry in this section) and then to describe the action that occurs between the family member and other people in the dream. After eliciting from the dreamer a good description of the family member and of his or her actions, we can then find out how this particular dream is a metaphor for something going on in the dreamer's current life, either in relation to this family member or to someone who is like the family member. At times we find that when an individual dreams of a mother or a sister the dream may be more about issues around motherhood and sisterhood than about a particular sister or a particular person in the dreamer's life. Again, it all depends upon the individual dream and the feelings it evokes at a particular time.

So many of us dream so frequently about our mothers and fathers that a special word is in order. If you are asked to describe your mother or your father, you could be talking for five or six hours. For the purposes of interpreting this particular dream, it's important to make your description fit the way your mother or father appeared in that dream. Are we talking about the generous or playful part of your mom, or are we talking about the more critical part of her? Your mother or father in a dream could represent issues in your relationship with that person or attitudes that you have incorporated from that person, such as things that you believe about yourself or the world simply because you were taught to believe them by your mother or your father. Or you might use your mother or father to represent certain traits in your current friends or lovers. Again, describe very carefully your mother and your father as he or she appears in the dream, and see how you can relate those traits to some part of yourself, to some situation in your life, or to someone else in your life.

SAMPLE DREAMS

Sis Is Gone

Theresa dreamt: "I was leaving my home in Boston to go to San Francisco and live with my sister, but when I arrived at the apartment my sister wasn't there. There was no sign of her, no trace, and I felt so lonely."

Theresa described her sister who, in fact, lives in New Mexico, as a very artistic woman who had enough courage to leave her East Coast academic world and become an artist in Santa Fe. Following her own drummer, her sister became a much happier person whom the dreamer admired. Theresa described San Francisco as a town perhaps less artsy than Santa Fe but nevertheless far more cosmopolitan and exciting, more international in flavor, and very progressive in politics. She thought it was probably the best place to live in the United States. When I asked her if she had any desire to move to a place that was more artistic, more sophisticated, more cosmopolitan, politically liberal, and exciting, she said yes indeed. Although she wasn't actually moving to San Francisco, she had begun to move in social circles that were much more like San Francisco than the traditional Boston cohorts she had known since college. In saying this, she suddenly realized the meaning of her dream. She said, "I've wanted to make a change the way my sister made a change. My goals are different from hers. I've tried to make this change, and I've tried to move into different circles; however, I'm not close to anyone there yet. It's as if I've moved closer to a sister or closer to sisterhood and female friendships, but I'm not really settled there yet."

Trouble

Edgar dreamt: "My brother is very angry at me. He is criticizing me and telling me I'm a selfish son of a bitch. Next scene: I see my mother in a coffin, and I wake up with a start."

Edgar had no trouble understanding his dream. He said that in waking life his brother had indeed called him a selfish son of a bitch for the last twenty years or so, but at the moment his brother was especially angry at him for not coming to visit his mother, who was in the hospital for eye surgery. Edgar thought phone contact was adequate and relied upon his brother to do the in-person attending to his mother since the brother lived near her. However, the coffin scene reminded him of how he would feel if his mother died and he had not gone back to see her. Instead of being his usual defensive self, saying, "Well, I can't come back because I'm so busy in my work," Edgar called his brother, told him he had been right, and announced he would be out to visit his mother within two weeks.

WHAT DO YOU SAY?

1. Describe the family member(s) in your dream. (See the people questions at the beginning of this section.)

2. How do you feel about this family member in waking life?

3. How do you feel about this family member in the dream?

4. Is there anyone in your life, other than this family member, or any part of yourself that is like your description?

5. Describe the dream action.

6. Describe your feelings in the dream.

7. Is the situation, including the people, the actions, and the feelings, similar to any situation in your waking life, now or in your childhood?

8. How so? Elaborate.

9. If the family member in the dream represents himself or herself, how does the dream comment on your relationship?

10. If the family member in the dream represents someone else in your life or some part of yourself, what new insights does this dream figure offer you?

A Young Child

VARIATIONS

It is amazing how vividly we can dream about young children. Often we don't know the children; sometimes they are ourselves or our own children at a younger age. Interestingly, often we know exactly how old the child is in our dream even if we know nothing else about him or her. The child may be helping us out, may be threatened or in pain, or may be a little wise one, giving us insight about our lives.

WHAT OTHERS HAVE SAID

A lot of silly things have been said about the meaning of young children in dreams. For example, Freud once wrote that beating children in a dream could be a symbol of masturbation. Most modern psychotherapists interpret the young child as an aspect of the dreamer's personality or as wishes to return to childhood or as a representation of immaturity in the adult dreamer. People sometimes dream of young children as representing young, not yet jaded parts of their own personality, vulnerable parts of themselves, neglected or endangered parts of themselves, unrealized potential, and so on. Another common interpretation is found by linking the child in the dream to some activity or project in the dreamer's life that is exactly as old as the child in the dream. For example, an eight-year-old child could represent the dreamer's eight-year marriage or career or an eight-year-long interest in growth or development.

SAMPLE DREAMS

Starving Three Year Old

Sandra dreamt that a three-year-old child who seemed to be hers in the dream was dying of starvation. She was horrified and awoke.

When we asked her to describe the three year old, she had little to say except that it was a pretty little baby who had been horribly neglected. We asked her if there was anything in her life that would be like a pretty little baby that was about three years old now and that had been badly neglected. She responded that she herself did not feel neglected but that she had started writing a book of poems three years earlier and in the last year or so had become discouraged and insecure about her own future as a poet so had let the project "waste away" on an obscure corner of her desk.

Thirteen Year Old

William dreamt of a thirteen-year-old boy who was tearing off his softball T-shirt, looking very unhappy and very angry.

We asked William to describe the boy. William said that he was athletic but sabotaging himself because his emotions were so strong; he was so upset that he couldn't play. Asked if he knew why the child was so upset, William responded, "The boy simply had so much inner conflict, probably trouble at home. He simply couldn't master his feelings enough to enjoy his own life." We asked him if there were anyone in his life or any part of himself like this. William said no, he wasn't aware of that. So then we asked him what he was like when he was thirteen. William said that was the year his parents announced a divorce, and in fact he did very badly in school that year, had regular temper tantrums, and didn't think anything was worth doing. We asked him why he might have had this dream right now in his life. Was there anything going on that might trigger the reanimation of these feelings he had experienced when he was only thirteen? William looked at us for just a moment and said, "My wife has announced that she wants a divorce, and I think inside I feel like that thirteen-year-old boy again, although it doesn't show."

WHAT DO YOU SAY?

1. Describe the child in your dream. What is the child like (describe his or her personality) and how is she or he feeling?
2. What is going on in the dream?
3. Is there any part of you that is like this little child?
4. How old is the child in the dream?
5. Is there any part of you, anyone in your life, or any project in your life that seems like this child and is the same "age"?
6. How might this dream be a parable about a current situation in your life?

Current Friends and Co-workers

VARIATIONS

Whenever I do a radio or TV show, producers and hosts love to tell me about their dreams of co-workers. Sometimes these are sexy dreams, and sometimes they're just funny ones. People tell of odd, surprising roles being played in their dreams by people they work with every day.

To understand these dreams, treat current friends and co-workers as you would any other dream person and get a good description. Then ask yourself what this person reminds you of in your current life. You may be dreaming about your work relationships, or you may be using these people as symbols for aspects of yourself or other people in your life. These dreams can be quite amusing, curious, or embarrassing. Usually people want to tell their friends and co-workers the dreams in which their friends have starring or supporting roles. Rarely is there harm in this except perhaps in situations where the person might give offense to the person dreamt about, as in highly sexual dreams.

WHAT OTHERS HAVE SAID

Traditional psychoanalysts often interpret contemporary co-workers and friends as being symbolic disguises for the dreamer's siblings—siblings with whom the dreamer is thought to want to have sexual encounters. Jungians often see these people as representing aspects of the dreamer's personality, although the more experienced Jungians often recognize that the dream may well be describing issues in the current relationship between the dreamer and the person dreamt about. Medard Boss, an existentialist and phenomenologist, in most cases interprets the dream friend or co-worker as an example of a way of being in the world to which the dreamer is open while dreaming.

I would add to these possibilities that it is important to note that if your friend or co-worker plays roles that are inimical to you—if, for instance, your boyfriend appears in your dreams time and again as a villain, a scoundrel, or a cold, distant person—you might be trying to tell yourself something that your friends could probably tell you but that you are resisting recognizing. If, on the other hand, your friends are trying to help you out in dreams, they often represent potential or actual personality traits or ways of being that could be extremely helpful to you in your waking life. If your therapist appears constantly in your dreams in a negative light, then it would behoove both of you to discuss the problems in your relationship. The dreams may not express a truth about the actual therapist, but at the very least you are dreaming about conflicts and negative feelings you have about this person or relationship. If you dream that a co-worker is constantly trying to do you in, however, it would be wise to interpret the dream first to see if you are dreaming about your relationship with your co-worker or about a part of your own personality or about someone close to you whom you see as malevolently disposed toward you. You may then be using a relatively unknown co-worker simply as a symbol for someone much closer to you.

SAMPLE DREAMS

Enough, Arthur!

Brian, a lawyer, dreamt: "I was with one of my partners at the firm, Arthur. We were at dinner, and he was drinking too much, as happens frequently, and I have been polite about it. In my dream I got very angry. I had had enough, I was sick of his drinking, and I told him he was going to ruin his life if he didn't get some help."

Brian described Arthur as a very able, handsome, good-hearted friend and law partner who indeed drank too much. Brian said neither he nor anyone else had confronted Arthur on the issue, and he thought maybe the dream was telling him it was time to confront Arthur. I decided to ask Brian one or two more questions. I asked, "Is there any part of yourself that is like Arthur, that's fun, able, a good law partner, a good friend, but who tends to drink too much and has not been confronted on it yet?" Brian said his wife told him that, but he felt he had his drinking under control. The dream offered him a moment to consider that perhaps he was in as much trouble as Arthur. The motif of a friend who drinks or takes drugs too much is a very common one in the dreams of overdrinkers and users who are in denial of their problems.

My Friend?

Melissa, a high school student, dreamt: "I am at school, and Inge is walking over my back. I'm sort of down on my hands and knees, and she is just walking over me. It doesn't feel very good."

When I asked Melissa to describe Inge she said, "Well, she's one of my closest friends at school, and she can be real difficult. She's critical of me, but we have fun together and she really wants me to be her best friend. So I do a lot of stuff with her, but she can be really difficult." I asked, "What is she doing in the dream?" Melissa answered, "She's walking over me. She's sort of using me to step on, sort of like a doormat." I asked, "Is there any way in your actual relationship with Inge that she uses you as a doormat, that she walks on top of you?" Melissa said, "Yes, she does, she does that a lot, and she expects me to just take it. I try to be a good friend, but she really can be a pain in the neck."

Melissa said that this dream made her recognize how inappropriately she was letting her so-called friend Inge walk all over her. She determined to address the issue with Inge and give her an ultimatum: "Either act like a friend, or don't ask to be a friend."

WHAT DO YOU SAY?

1. Describe the friend or co-worker in your dream as he or she is in waking life. Who is he or she, and what is he or she like? Give at least three adjectives describing that person's personality.
2. What is your friend or co-worker doing in the dream?
3. What is this friend or co-worker like in the dream?
4. How are you feeling in the dream about your friend?
5. Is there any situation in your life that this dream scenario reminds you of?
6. Is there anyone in your life besides the pictured friend or co-worker who fits this description?
7. What insight does your dream offer you either about your relationship with this particular friend or with the part of yourself or other person in your life the dream character resembles?

Your Enemies

VARIATIONS

In all of our lives there are people we just don't like. In fact, most of us have one or two we really can't stand. If we're really lucky, there are only one or two who actually act as our enemies. It's not usually very pleasant to dream of one of your enemies or least beloved friends, but it does happen, and it happens for a reason. Usually your enemy is doing something obnoxious in the dream, such as causing you trouble, threatening you, or endangering you. Other times your dream enemies lead you to reexperience feelings familiar in waking life, such as feelings of being laughed at, of being left out, or of being criticized. A surprising variation in this dream is one in which you dream of an enemy who is helping you out, who in the dream actually has something to offer you and is trying to help you.

WHAT OTHERS HAVE SAID

Dream enemies have been interpreted by psychoanalysts through the years as disguised representations of the dreamer's parents or the dreamer's therapist, and so forth. Jung emphasized that dream enemies can represent the shadow side of your personality—a part of yourself that you reject, that you do not admit to having, but that, once understood, can actually enrich both your personality and your tolerance of others. I would say that while all these interpretations can certainly be true, your dream enemies can also provide vivid pictures of the quality of your relationship with the person pictured in your dream. Again, the only way you're going to find out what your dream enemy means to you is to describe that person and his or her dream actions as if you were describing them to someone from another planet who has never heard of such a person before. When you restate that description to yourself, it should sound familiar and help you to bridge the dream scenario to your waking life.

SAMPLE DREAMS

Angry at Neighbor

Amy, who at the time was in the midst of a four-year lawsuit with a neighbor, dreamt: "My neighbor Graham had parked his car on my front lawn. I was furious at the intrusion. I called him over to my front porch. I told him he had no right to do such a thing. How dare he be so intrusive, come through my gate, and park his car? Graham, acting innocent and smiling, said, 'Why, I haven't done anything, why would you be angry with me?' I was so angry that I pushed him up against the wall, slapped him across the face, threw him down on the ground, twisted his arm behind his back, and said, 'You won't even admit your aggression toward me, you won't even admit it, you act so innocent!' I woke up furious."

In describing her neighbor, Amy said she experienced him as a very selfish, spoiled person who always wanted to get his way no matter what discomfort it cost anyone around him and that he was very aggressive. Meanwhile, he thought he was the wronged party. "The funny thing was," she said, "that in the midst of the dream as I was screaming and roughing up my neighbor, Graham, he was smiling and talking very much the way my husband does." The fact that he looked like her husband in the dream forced her to see how much her husband acts in similar ways. "My husband's aggression is less overt than my neighbor's, but both of them deny that they are the aggressors. Just getting them to admit their intrusiveness would give me some satisfaction, because both of them have been so intrusive in my life."

Friend Steals Wine

Henriette dreamt: "I was in my kitchen when Christina rang my doorbell. She came in, and without saying a word she took all the red wine out of my closet and left."

Henriette was a member of one of our weekly dream study groups and was being interviewed by an apprentice interviewer. To describe Christina, Henriette said, "She is a pretty, bright, sexy woman, but she is very self-centered and doesn't seem to be able to grasp the larger picture when it comes to her actions in her relationships or her work." Asked if there was anyone in her life like her, Henriette said, "No, just Christina." Then the interviewer asked her to describe red wine. Henriette said she loves red wine and the red wine in her closet was her husband's favorite, cabernet. Our interviewer asked, "Is there any situation in your life in which someone like Christina, who is very self-centered, sexy, and talented, takes your husband's favorite red wine out of the house?" Henriette said, "Well, I guess that could be a picture of the part of myself that's having an affair. I haven't told my husband, but in a sense I'm taking his favorite wine out of the house, in that my most intense sexual fantasies and interest are not there for him anymore. Then I suppose it's very self-centered of me, but, you know, I just got tired of waiting for him to get more interesting, to be more exciting. I took matters into my own hands, and I suppose that's been pretty selfish of me. The only alternative would have been to drag him, kicking and screaming, into psychotherapy or couples' counseling."

WHAT DO YOU SAY?

1. Describe the enemy in your dream. What is he or she like? What is he or she doing in your dream?

2. Is there anyone in your life or any part of yourself that is like this dream enemy and that is doing something analogous to what is going on in the dream?

3. How so? Elaborate on the connection to see if it is a strong one.

4. If you think your dream enemy represents a part of yourself, what would you like to do about it?

5. If you think the dream enemy represents someone in your life you have seen very negatively, do you think it would be appropriate to discuss the matter with this person?

6. If you think the dream enemy represents the actual person pictured in the dream, what do you think you could do about the relationship to improve it?

3 Dream Settings

How to Interpret Any Dream Setting

Here are the basic dream interview questions you can ask yourself about any setting in your dreams in order to discover why you dreamt of being in Texas or in Paris or at Uncle Fred's house. Your dream setting is never coincidental, and it can serve to set the tone and to indicate the part of your life under discussion in your dream. Remember, as you interview yourself or a friend, the dream interviewer pretends to come from another planet and has no idea what Texas is like or who your Uncle Fred is. Instead, he or she asks you to give a precise description of the setting, which will include how you feel about the setting both in waking life and in the dream. Feel free to add to, modify, or even skip questions when it seems appropriate. Just be sure to get a definitive description of the setting before you try to interpret its meaning.

1. Describe the opening (or the next) setting of the dream as if I come from another planet and need to know its nature and function.
2. What is this place like in your dream?
3. Is it different from such a place in waking life? How?
4. How does it feel to be in this setting?
5. So this setting is (restate the description). Right?
6. Does this setting, which you describe as (restate the description again), remind you of any situation or area in your waking life?
7. How so? Elaborate to be sure there is a good metaphorical fit.

Your Parents', Grandparents', or a Relative's Home

VARIATIONS

You probably can remember many dreams that took place at the home of someone you used to visit in your childhood. Perhaps it was the home of a grandmother, an aunt, an uncle, or your neighbor's home. Perhaps it was your parents' home. You may be a child again in the dream, but more likely you are your current age following adventures that unfold on the porch, in the kitchen, upstairs in the bedroom, or anywhere in and around the house. The dreams can be pleasant or unpleasant, but usually they are simply curious dreams. You wonder, why was I back there again? Let's take a look at how others have answered that question.

WHAT OTHERS HAVE SAID

You can still find psychoanalysts who interpret dreams that take place in a home you visited in childhood as a regression to childhood and a desire to return to the mother. Most people today, however, pay attention to what was going on in the dream setting and look for a trigger in your current life that causes you to reexperience certain feelings that you associate with this home from your past. Most analysts ask a dreamer what was going on in the childhood home and what feelings they experienced during the dream. Then they look to see what current life circumstances might be triggering these feelings, which might have had their origins in childhood.

If you are dreaming of your childhood home, you would want to focus on the years you lived in that house because it's highly probable that the issues the dream is dealing with had their origin in that particular period of your life. When dreaming of a particular person's house, I think it is useful to be even more specific and to use the questions under "People in Dreams" to first get a good description of the person to whom the house belongs. For example, if you dream of Aunt Matilda's house, you would want to know who Aunt Matilda is and what she was like when you knew her as well as in what period of your life you visited her home. You would want to have a good description of Aunt Matilda, to find out if the attitudes and ways of living pictured by Aunt Matilda's house are relevant in your life right now. If going to visit your mother-in-law, for example, feels like going back to visit rigid, strict, unloving Aunt Matilda, you can imagine why you would dredge up the memory of Aunt Matilda to dream about your relationship with your in-laws. If, on the other hand, Aunt Matilda was a warm, loving person who understood you when no one else could, she might remind you of your current husband and how good it feels to go home to him, or you may find that being with your best friend is very much like being with Aunt Matilda. As you can see, it all depends on how you answer your own questions.

SAMPLE DREAMS

Grandmother's House

Tanna dreamt: "I was back at my grandmother's house as an adult, and I was wondering where I would sleep tonight. When I asked my grandmother and she told me that I could sleep anywhere I wanted, I was shocked because she was always so compulsive she would have planned everything down to the last detail. I rather liked her relaxed style. Then I woke up."

We asked Tanna to describe her grandmother, who had died fifteen years earlier. Tanna said that her grandmother had been a very rigid woman, very loving, but a woman who tended to alienate the people close to her because she was so controlling. "Even when she tried to celebrate a happy holiday event," Tanna said, "we would dread going there because it was sort of like going to a happy police state, but a police state nevertheless." Asked if there were any part of her own personality or anyone in her life who was like her grandmother, Tanna said, "Well, I guess you could say that I have become like that. I have four children, and I even dread my own Thanksgivings. I get them planned out in great detail, I make sure that everyone will have plenty to eat and the right place to sleep, but I think I'm too heavy-handed like my grandmother." Asked how she felt in the dream, Tanna said that she was surprised at her grandmother's relaxed style, and she commented to her dream group members that perhaps it was time for her to relax and not worry that everything would fall apart if she failed to control every single moment of the day. She said her grandmother would have been fantastic if she just could have relaxed a little.

Home Bombs

David dreamt that he was back in his childhood home when he heard two bombs going off. He ran upstairs to find his wife when he heard the third bomb. He woke up with a start.

David said that the flavor of his childhood home, which he lived in until he was out of high school, was one of constant upheaval and anger, with parents who had regular shouting matches. He said that the bombs in the dream reminded him a great deal of the fights and of his waiting for the next bomb to drop and the next fight to start. In the dream, David was his own age and he wanted to escape the house with his wife. Asked if there were anything going on in his current life that was like this situation, David said that he and his wife were having shouting matches just like his parents, and he thought the dream expressed his desire to "get us both the hell out of there." David was giving himself a strong dream message to do something about his relationship with his wife, in which he was repeating patterns from childhood.

WHAT DO YOU SAY?

1. Describe the house in your dream. What years of your life did you live in or visit that household?
2. Describe the personality of the person whose house you are dreaming about.
3. Is there anyone in your life or any part of yourself that is like the owner of your dream house?

4. Try to remember the major issues going on in your life during the time you lived in that house or visited it regularly.

5. Describe the action that occurs in the dream. Is there any situation in your current life that is like the action in the dream and that takes place when you act or feel like the owner of the house?

6. Is there any situation in your current life that is similar to the issues that were going on at the time you lived in or visited that house?

7. Describe the major people, actions, and feelings that occur during this dream and ask yourself, What current life situation could bring these memories back to life?

8. Does this dream help you identify patterns of behavior learned in childhood that you are now repeating to your own benefit or detriment in your adult life?

A Church or School

VARIATIONS

Have you dreamt of being back at your old grammar school or high school or university? Maybe you were in the gymnasium or a particular classroom or homeroom. Or have you dreamt of being back at a language school or a trade school you attended? In your dreams you may also have visited a childhood church or a particular church that in waking life you have never entered. There may be parties going on at the school or the church, you may be meeting particular people, or you may be listening to a lecture or sermon. Whatever is taking place in the school or church, you certainly are having certain feelings about it in the dream.

WHAT OTHERS HAVE SAID

Carl Jung saw some church dreams as representing the spiritual concerns of people, perhaps their conflicts with organized religions and churches or simply their exploration of the spirit in their own development. Some psychoanalysts consider a church as a return to the mother and a return to school as a return to times of adolescence and budding sexuality, or they may see dreams of school or church as a simple desire to regress to childhood and escape from the complications of adult life. I have never seen regression as the main theme in a church or school dream, although I could certainly imagine that might occur. What seems much more common is that people dream of a particular place or time in their lives because something happened the day before the dream that triggered associated feelings, hopes, anxieties, or concerns.

SAMPLE DREAMS

Dinner in Church

Tina dreamt: "I walked into a church and sat down for dinner. It was like being in a soap opera. Everyone was complaining and crying about how sad their lives were, how much trouble they were having, or how sinful they were. I found it very depressing and woke up."

I asked Tina to describe the kind of church she went into. She said, "Well, it was some Protestant church that emphasized pain, suffering, and guilt." I asked if anywhere in her life she felt that she was in an environment like that, and she said that actually her home life was painfully similar. For the last couple of years she had been acting like the ultimate victim. She had many children and felt overwhelmed by the responsibilities. She usually thought of herself as following a strict, Calvinist-Protestant, stiff-upper-lip way of living, and yet the dream helped her see she spent most of her time complaining. She thought the dream was a perfect picture of a very depressing way of life full of complaining. Tina said she would much rather live her religion in a more grateful celebration of the Christian tradition. Now she had to ask herself how she could manage her life and her attitude about it differently.

I Can Dance

Rosemary dreamt: "I'm back in my high school gymnasium, and there is some party going on, probably a dance. I'm worried that no one will ask me to dance. I feel awkward and relatively powerless to do anything about the situation since in those days girls did not ask boys to dance. I hated it! I woke up."

I asked what high school was like and what high school dances were like as if I had never heard of them before. Rosemary said that they were a chance to start dating, a low-key, easy way, but a way that ended up being nerve-wracking because girls were put in the awkward position of having to wait for the boys to ask them to dance. The boys were often shy, so that everyone at the dance felt slightly miserable and anxious until later in the party when things livened up. I asked if this situation reminded her of any place in her life where she felt like she was back at a high school dance again. Rosemary laughed and said she had been divorced only a few months and was just now starting to date. She said it felt very much like being back in high school, where she knew she would have to wait a while for the ball to get rolling; right now she was feeling shy, anxious, and a little angry that she couldn't call a man and ask him for a date as easily as he could call her. She knew that it was "all right" for a woman to ask a man out, but from her friends' experience she had learned that it almost always worked better if, as in the high school dance, the woman did whatever it took to attract the man to make the first move. This dream gave Rosemary another perspective on her current anxiety as well as a little humor and a little more patience.

WHAT DO YOU SAY?

1. Describe the church or the school in your dream.
2. What was going on in this setting? Give at least three adjectives describing how you felt in the dream situation.
3. Is there any situation in your life where you feel the way you felt in the dream?
4. Is there any place in your life that feels like the high school or the church in your dream?
5. What has happened in the last couple of days that might have given rise to this dream experience?

A Particular Town, State, or Country

VARIATIONS

Isn't it wonderful how vividly you can travel to fascinating places in your dreams? You might dream of being in Santa Fe, New Mexico, or in a city in Africa or perhaps on a mountaintop in the Himalayas. The dream paints the scene for you with all the feeling of the familiarity or the strangeness of the place that you choose to dream about on that particular night. You may see local people in your dream, or you may be a local yourself. You may be in this particular place with people from your hometown, or you may meet exotic strangers who themselves are traveling from place to place. In any case, the particular location you choose for your dream sets a tone and often identifies the area of your life your dream is going to deal with.

WHAT OTHERS HAVE SAID

Many therapists interpret the setting in your dream according to their own impressions of the place, and if these impressions are close to your own no harm may be done. If, however, these impressions are significantly different, the dream interpretation will suffer. In our dream center classes we have lots of fun figuring out what a particular town, state, or country in our dreams means. If we ask five people to describe the same place, say the state of Texas— what it's like and what kinds of people live there—we get such a variety of responses that it becomes clear to everyone in the class that only the dreamer can give us the relevant answers.

SAMPLE DREAMS

Before reading this dream, let me invite you to write down on a piece of paper a two- or three-line description of the state of New Hampshire. What kind of state is it, what kinds of people live there, and how do you like it? Then take a look at Pia's dream to see how her description compares with yours.

Far Away to New Hampshire

Pia dreamt: "I am on a plane headed for New Hampshire because, it turns out, that's where my boyfriend is from and I'm going to meet his family and to try to understand his lifestyle. That's all I remember of the dream."

When a dream group member asked Pia to describe New Hampshire she said, "It's the furthest part of the United States away from my home in San Francisco, the furthest part away geographically, morally, and spiritually. It's very far away. New Hampshire people are very, very straight, they're stuck, they are moralistic, and they tend to be older and of course very, very conservative. Independent, and I like that part, but all the rest would be very stifling to me." Asked if the attitude that Pia associates with New Hampshire describes the origins of the family of her boyfriend, she said she was afraid so. Pia felt the dream was making her look at this highly improbable match because she said that if indeed her new boyfriend turns out to be like her view of New Hampshire people, then even his good looks, good humor, and high intelligence would not be enough to overcome such a fundamental mismatch.

Sophisticated San Francisco

I once dreamt of seeing the Golden Gate Bridge at different times of day, sunrise to sunset. I saw the daylight changing, the fog coming in, and the mist. The whole dream simply consisted of appreciating the beauty and the grace of the bridge and these constantly changing scenes and atmospheres. As I dreamt the dream I understood that the bridge symbolized something I shared with my new boyfriend—a sense of grace, elegance, and changing lights, for want of a better word. I woke up delighted by the dream.

In interviewing myself I asked, "What is the Golden Gate Bridge like?" The answer was that to me the bridge over the San Francisco Bay is one of the most beautiful places on earth; the Bay Area feels like my homeland, not a foreign country, and the bridge that connects the San Francisco Peninsula with Marin County to the north connects the excitement of city life with suburban country life. The very special thing about this place is that it never stays the same. The weather changes all the time, the light changes, the view of this area is so varied that it's forever fascinating—sometimes restful, sometimes exciting, but always beautiful. I realized that my description of the bridge articulated some of the special qualities I thought possible with my new boyfriend. He had both the sophistication of the city and the appreciation of the country. His personality was both mature enough to be varied and wise, yet exciting and young enough to be always interesting. I dreamt of the Golden Gate Bridge and not other lovely bridges and bodies of water to emphasize the fact that there was no lack of excitement with this man even though he lives near my hometown. The aesthetic pleasure in the dream is one I associate very strongly with San Francisco and in fact describes my aesthetic connection with this man.

WHAT DO YOU SAY?

1. Describe the place in your dreams as if you are describing it to a person from another planet who has never heard of it before. Use at least three adjectives.

2. Do you like or dislike this place? What kinds of people tend to live here? Give your impression, not just the facts.

3. How does it feel to be in this setting in the dream?

4. Is there any area of your life or any relationship in your life that feels like this setting?

5. How does this setting highlight certain aspects of your current life?

Buildings

VARIATIONS

When a building in your dream gets your attention, it is important to interpret it. You may dream of being in an old warehouse or in a familiar or unfamiliar house, in skyscrapers or colonial office buildings, in the town hall, in police stations, train stations, airports, TV stations, hotels, motels, bars, restaurants, palaces, or poorhouses.

WHAT OTHERS HAVE SAID

Some orthodox Freudians still cling to the interpretation of a building as a body, its entrances as orifices. Modern analysts appreciate the myriad things buildings can represent in dreams, and they take careful note of the type of building, its condition, and, of course, the action that takes place within it. For example, if you find yourself in a house with your wife noticing that the foundations are crumbling or that it is rat infested, you might ask yourself how this could be a description of your relationship or some other joint venture.

SAMPLE DREAM

Delta Delight Lounge

Kirk dreamt: "I'm at an airport frantically trying to find the Delta terminal. I'm afraid I'm going to miss the plane, and I'm rushing. I ask everyone, 'Which way is the terminal?' People start to laugh when I ask them the way, and they say, 'You don't want to fly Delta.' I press through the crowds, running, running, then I pass a beautiful girl who puts her hand on my face and says, 'I feel so bad that you are going to miss your flight.' I reply, 'Well, if I do, where will you be?' She says she'll be in the TV lounge."

I asked Kirk to describe airports. He replied that in general airports are fun and exciting places that lead you to new and different adventures. I asked him what the Delta terminal was like. He said, "Well, I never fly Delta. I fly other airlines because I have my mileage on those, but I hear that Delta is probably a better company with better programs. In my dream I really want to fly Delta." I asked, "Is there anything in your life that you want the way you want to fly Delta?" He responded, "Well, I don't know why, but I think of dating really beautiful women, like models, but I don't usually go after them because I don't think they will be attracted to me." I asked Kirk to describe the woman who put her hand on his face and said she was sorry he was going to miss his flight. Kirk said, "She was beautiful, was just gorgeous. In fact, she picked me out of the crowd." When she told him she'd be in the TV lounge he thought, "Oh, this is too good to be true. I could easily find the TV lounge." I asked him to describe TV lounges, pretending I'd never heard of them before. He said, "They're easy, comfortable places to be, and this gorgeous woman was going to be right there." Before he knew it, Kirk was describing his way of seeking out great women. He had always been attracted to the high-profile, trophy women, which in his dream were the Delta women. He had been planning to find the Delta terminal, but he also knew that that sort of woman was rarely attracted to him. The surprise in the dream was that this gorgeous woman had sought him out and could be found in an easy, comfortable environment. It gave him some confidence that maybe he could find a wonderful woman, even a gorgeous woman, if he would just relax and live his life the way he was comfortable living it and question his belief that gorgeous women are to be found only in jet-set environments.

WHAT DO YOU SAY?

1. Describe the building in your dream. What is its function, what is its condition, and how do you feel about it?

2. Describe the action in your dream. How do you feel being in this building or trying to get to this building?

3. Is there any situation in your current life or in your past where you feel or have felt the way you do in this dream?

4. How so? Elaborate.

5. How do your descriptions of the building and the feelings you have about the building match a certain circumstance in your life or a certain area of your life?

6. How does the action that takes place in your dream building shed light on a situation in your current life?

Prisons

VARIATIONS

Many people dream of being sentenced to prison and of being in prison, of trying to escape from prison, of being in prisons that are lovely but deadly places, of being in horribly frightening prisons. People dream of getting to know their prison guards, of loving them or hating them.

WHAT OTHERS HAVE SAID

As you can imagine, the traditional dream dictionaries emphasize that being in prison is a bad omen. It might indicate obstacles and difficulties as well as, Artemidorus tells us, the future illness of one's wife. Psychoanalysts generally see prisons as expressing the dreamer's emotional repression or the dreamer's self-limitations or limitations within the context of career or relationships. Jungians have matched the image of prisons with excessive introversion as well a desire for solitude and meditation. Several other interpreters look to prisons as a sign of the dreamer's sense of guilt, appropriate or not. I have seen prisons represent many things for people, including the feelings one has in a relationship, in a job, in a family setting, or in general life circumstances. Being in prison has never been described to me as a happy experience but rather one of restrictions, limitations, and discontent.

Among my clients' dreams, the single most common use I have seen made of the image of prison is to express the dreamer's feeling—and it's usually the female dreamer's feeling—that she is in prison in the context of a limiting marriage or romantic relationship. When women dream of prison guards and then describe the personalities and behaviors of the prison guards in the dream, they often discover that they are describing their own husbands or boyfriends. This does not necessarily mean that the husband or boyfriend is in fact acting as a prison guard, although it might. It can also mean that the dreamer, through her own needs for security or because of simple habits from childhood, has set up a relationship in which she feels imprisoned, unfree, and very limited.

SAMPLE DREAMS

Sentenced to Solitary Confinement

I once dreamt that I had just been sentenced to four or five years of solitary confinement. In the dream I reflect, "Well, that's not so bad; at least I'll get a lot of reading done and learn a lot."

When I interviewed myself about this theme I described solitary confinement as a dreadful, lonely experience. The only thing that could be said for such an experience is that one could indeed, with a great deal of discipline, learn a lot during that period. But as I interviewed myself about the dream my emotional response was, "Not on your life! I could die before four or five years are up, and that's how long I would have to go to a conservative graduate school to get my Ph.D. in psychology." I decided at that very moment not to apply to the schools I had been thinking about on the East Coast but rather to get my degree from an avant-garde school that would allow me to study psychology and dreams in a more open and creative environment. I refused to spend the next four or five years of my life keeping my interest in modernizing the study of dreaming a secret while I pretended to be interested in more traditional areas of the field.

Held Hostage

Susie dreamt: "Nan, my best friend, is being held hostage by some Mafia types in a house across the street. She calls to tell me about it and begs for help. I immediately call the police and then run over to the house to tell the bad guys I've already called and it's too late for their threats. They are about to inject me with a drug. Oh, dear, the situation could still be very dangerous if I lose my focus."

Susie interviewed herself about Nan, asking, "Who is Nan and what is Nan like?" She thought, "Nan is my best friend, she is very smart, very capable, but she has a difficult time with men." Then she asked herself, "What is Nan like in my dreams?" She responded, "Nan is very much the way she actually was in waking life about five years ago when she called me to tell me that her husband was threatening to kill her. Nan is a woman who has been known to get herself into an abusive relationship because she was unwilling to see the warning signs soon enough. That reminds me of myself, because just last night I wrote in my journal that I was worried about my boyfriend's drinking and about his vindictiveness—he feels justified in being mean to people who have wronged him or who have hurt his feelings. I like to think that my situation with my boyfriend is not as dire as Nan's was with her husband, but my dream draws a direct parallel. I think of Nan as a part of myself whom I have to save. The threat of being injected in the dream reminds me of sex, which I can use as a drug. My sexy boyfriend could make me lose my focus and forget to take care of myself."

WHAT DO YOU SAY?

1. Describe the prison situation in your dream. If you know why you were sentenced or why you were sent there, include this in your description.

2. What are prisons like? Pretend I've never heard of them before. What is the prison in your dream like?

3. Describe the personality or the role of anyone else in the dream, including fellow inmates, prison keepers, and guards.

4. Describe how you feel about being in prison, being sent to prison, or about the people in the dream.

5. Is there any place in your life where you feel like you are in prison and unfree?

6. Is there any situation in your life where you feel the same way as you feel in the dream?

7. How so? Elaborate.

8. Is there anyone in your life or any part of yourself that is like the prison guard or prison keeper in your dream?

9. How so? Elaborate.

10. How do the feelings of the people and the actions in your prison dream remind you of a current or past situation in your life?

11. Do you want to get out of this prison, and if so, how?

The Desert and Dry, Barren Places

VARIATIONS

Frequently people tell of being in a dry, barren desert in their dreams or of being in a dry playground or a place where nothing much is growing. These are not the desert dreams of people who love the desert and talk about the spring flowers and beautiful sunsets but rather dreams that focus on the dryness and the barrenness of the place. Any kind of action can take place in these settings, but often the dreamer tells of simply walking in such an environment with a husband or a wife or a little child.

WHAT OTHERS HAVE SAID

You probably will not be surprised to hear that some analysts interpret desert dreams as expressing hopes or fears of biological barrenness (on the part of female dreamers) or (if the male is dreaming) concern that one's seed will be sterile. Most modern analysts interpret these dreams as having to do with a quality of dryness or barrenness in the dreamer's current life. Usually all it takes to interpret this image is asking the dreamer to describe this dry environment and then feeding back this description with the question, "Is there anywhere in your life it feels dry and barren like the place in your dream?" Most dreamers can quickly pinpoint that part of their lives, and, sadly, for some dreamers such a description fits their feeling about their entire lives.

SAMPLE DREAMS

The Desert Trip

Colette dreamt: "I am traveling through a desert with a group of friends. Hills. Desolate surroundings. The feeling is of adventure and some seriousness. This trip could be depressing, but it is going fine, so there is nothing to get upset about."

Colette described a desert as an almost endless, dry, dull barrenness. When we asked her how it felt to be in the desert in her dream she said, "It feels endless. I'm not sure we have a mission; the important thing is the travel. It's a terrible journey. I'm glad to be with friends. It's plodding. It's desolate." We asked her if she could bridge these feelings and this setting to any situation in her life, and she said that her daily life felt like this. Her work was unsatisfying, she had to move—in itself a lot of work—and also she had an enormous amount of work to do on her psychological growth to recover from early childhood abuse. She said she felt as if she was relentlessly plodding, and yet in the dream there was some excitement of being aware, of knowing that terrible things could happen but that even though this could be depressing it could also be exciting. She said this clearly described her experience in her journey to heal herself from her childhood wounds. As usual, the setting of Colette's dream was just the opening part of a very long dream. Simply understanding the desert and how she felt within it placed the dream in the context of her life and helped her focus on her sense of fatigue and desolation mixed with excitement in her important but very difficult psychological work.

Bored with My Wife

Joseph dreamt: "I was walking in the desert with my wife. We were holding hands, she was talking, I was bored."

I asked Joseph to describe a desert in general. He said that he thought of a desert as a dry place where nothing grows. When I asked him what his desert in his dream felt like, he said, "It felt just like that." I asked Joseph to describe the desert, what it was like to be in the desert in his dream. He said, "Well, it was boring and nothing was growing and it felt very barren." I asked him how it felt to be walking with his wife. He said, "Dull." I asked, "Is there anything going on in your life that feels like a dull walk with your wife in a very barren place?" Joseph said, "My marriage. Neither of us has done anything new lately. Neither of us brings anything new to the relationship, and life seems excruciatingly dull. One reason I joined the dream group is to bring at least the excitement of my dreams into my life. What the dream makes me realize, though, is that I'm just as guilty as my wife. I'm walking down the path in the desert with as little excitement as she. I don't think of anything new; we're both in this together."

WHAT DO YOU SAY?

1. Describe the desert or dry place in your dream. First give a generic description of such places, then describe the one in your dream.

2. Describe each of the people who appear in the dream. (See people questions in the section "People in Dreams.")

3. How does it feel to be in this place with these people?

4. Is there any situation in your life in which you feel the way you do in your dream?

5. How so? Elaborate.

6. Does the stark representation of the desert in your dream and its connectedness to the situation in your life help you to see anything more clearly?

7. Is there anything you want to do or can do about the fact that this part of your life feels like a desert?

Paradisiacal Settings

VARIATIONS

These are the dreams of milk and honey, of reflecting ponds and waterfalls and lush gardens. Sometimes we're lucky enough to dream of being in paradise or to be in places that fill us with the joy of luscious, verdant surroundings. Things may go well, even very romantically, in a paradisiacal dream. But just as frequently we discover there is trouble in paradise. There may be villains after us or tidal waves about to swallow us up or evil influences that are difficult to identify but nevertheless are present and threatening. A storm may come and threaten to destroy us, or we may simply be having a terrible argument with a family member in the middle of a luscious dream world.

WHAT OTHERS HAVE SAID

Some psychoanalysts see paradisiacal dreams as expressing a wish to return to the womb and to the days of carefree childhood. Some Jungians interpret such dreams as returning to the source of the self, to the growing center of the individual. Others see this dream as expressing a part of the dreamer's life that is going very well or, if there is trouble in paradise, a part of life that's going very well but contains a bit of trouble. The problems in paradise may represent certain self-sabotaging, self-destructive attitudes or behaviors on the part of the dreamer. They might also represent difficult relationships that keep the dreamer from enjoying the sweetness of life. One way to discover the meaning of these problems in paradise is, of course, to ask the dreamer to describe the setting and the people carefully.

SAMPLE DREAMS

Ignoring Rough Seas

Adam dreamt: "I was in Hawaii. The palm trees were swaying, the beach was warm, the water was sparkling, the sky was brilliant, and I was having the time of my life. I went on my surfboard and took a couple of waves, and then I saw that there was a storm warning but I decided to take one more wave. I got out pretty far, the wind picked up, the storm started, and I thought, 'Oh, oh, I should have come in at the first warning.' The seas were very rough suddenly, and I knew I was going to have a hard time getting back to shore."

Adam described this setting and said it reminded him of his life two years after completing school. He had a wonderful job and a fabulous girlfriend and was very happy with his life. I asked him, "What is it like to ignore a warning for rough seas?" He said, "Well, you can usually get away with it for a while." But in the dream he had pushed his luck too far and was risking very rough seas. I asked if there was anywhere in his life right now that was paradisiacal, where everything was wonderful, but where he might be pushing his luck too far and ignoring the warnings. He said his friends had been warning him lately that he was doing something very stupid by dating two women in the same office where he worked. He thought he could get away with it, but the dream made him wonder if he might be pushing his luck too far.

Roman Spas

Julie dreamt: "I was in the countryside at a spa near ancient Rome. It was incredibly beautiful and warm. There were glorious pools everywhere with lounge chairs all around. Lengths of fabric shaded us from the sun; people were drinking wine and eating fruit, lounging, sensual. I was with a man who was Adonis incarnate. We were kissing and soon we were making love, right there, and no one seemed to mind. Adonis said to me, 'You're so hot!' I looked down at him and said, 'I know.' It was a fantastic dream, it was sexy, it was comfortable, it was paradise."

We asked Julie to describe ancient Rome and the spas around it. She said, "Ancient Rome had lots of trouble, but one of the things they knew how to do well was create beautiful spas and sensuous environments." We asked her to describe her particular spa and how it felt to be there. She said it was "both comfortable to the body and to the psyche, very sensual, and not at all threatening" to her. "Never before this dream have I felt so comfortable with my own sexuality." She thought the dream provided a setting for her to make a breakthrough that came first in her dream but that she said also moved her to a new level in waking life.

WHAT DO YOU SAY?

1. Describe the paradisiacal setting in your dream. How does it feel to be in this setting?

2. Describe the action that takes place in your dream. How do you feel about this action?

3. Do these feelings remind you of anything going on in your current life?

4. How so? Elaborate.

5. Can you relate this setting to any aspect of your life?

6. Is there anyone else in the dream? If so, describe that person. (See how to describe people in the section "People in Dreams.")

7. Is there anyone in your life or any part of your self like the people in your dream? Could the people in your dream represent a type of person?

8. How does the setting and the action within this setting, including the people in the dream, picture a current situation in your life?

4 Animals in Dreams

How to Interpret Any Animal in Your Dreams

Whatever animal you dream about, a few basic questions will help you unlock the meaning you invest in that image. It's extremely helpful to consider what you imagine to be the personality of your dream animal—what its personality is like in waking life and what its traits are in your dream. The meaning of the dream animal for you will be determined by how the animal acts, how it looks, and how you feel about the animal in the context of the dream.

The examples of specific animals, which follow below, will give you an idea of how to work with specific images. All you have to do is modify your questions to the animal you dream about, no matter how unusual or bizarre the animal is.

Here are the interview questions that will help you interpret any animal in your dreams. Remember to ask these questions as if you, in the role of interviewer, come from another planet and have no preconceptions about the image. Then, in answering the question, remember that you are speaking to someone who comes from another planet and is unfamiliar with your particular web of associations and impressions. Just give as direct and as informative an answer as you can to the extraterrestrial who really is only interested in knowing what *you* think about the images in your dream.

1. What is this animal like? Pretend I've never seen one before.

2. How would you describe the personality of this type of animal?

3. What is the animal doing in your dream?

4. Is there anyone in your life or anything or any part of yourself that is like this animal, which you describe as (restate the description)?

5. How so? Test the bridge, or connection, to your waking life by elaborating on the similarities.

Cats

VARIATIONS

People dream of cats that are healthy, cats that are starved for attention or for food, cats that are mistreated, cats that are lost, cats that act in certain surprising ways. Dream cats have been known to wreak havoc in a bedroom, play hard to get, suffer and cry out "love me, love me," and, of course, to bite and attack the dreamer. Sometimes the cats are orange, sometimes they look like a cat as well as another animal, sometimes they limp, sometimes they gracefully leap over a fence. There seems to be no end to the various roles cats can play in dreams.

WHAT OTHERS HAVE SAID

The psychoanalyst Alexander Grinstein describes cats, in good Freudian style, as a common symbol for the female genitals, often because of the play on the word *pussy*. But, with a healthy respect for his patients' associations, he goes on to note that the cat can have many different meanings. He once had a patient who dreamt of a cat lying curled up on a couch. The patient's associations revealed that the dreamer had been planning to take the family tomcat to the vet to have him neutered and declawed. The analyst's interpretation was that the dreamer identified himself with the tomcat and the analyst was like the veterinarian who would castrate the dreamer; the dream thus described some of the dreamer's anxiety in his therapeutic relationship. Jungians frequently consider cats to be symbols of the feminine. The Jungian Karen Signell adds that what makes a cat a special symbol is that it represents an independence of the unconscious from our control; the unconscious is wild like the cat that cannot be tamed. She also sees the cat as representing instincts both good and bad, which she sees as neglected parts of feminine nature. She adds that the cat defines itself and maintains its individuality no matter what its owner commands. Signell says, "The cat has represented contemplative wisdom, the good mother who nurtures her young, playfulness, cruelty, and, above all, the independent feminine spirit."[1]

I think it is difficult to define what *feminine* means to different people at different times of their lives and in different times of history. I tend to look at a cat without assuming that it has any connection to anything feminine. I prefer to ask the dreamer to describe the cat, and then I follow the dreamer. My clients have told me about vicious cats that remind them of their mothers and wild tomcats that remind them of their fathers. Others have told me of cats who are neglected and starved, which they have then associated with the parts of themselves that have felt neglected, either as children or as adults. Thus it is very important to look at the specific cat in your dreams—how you feel about it, the condition of the cat in the dream, the cat's actions, and your feeling about the particular cat you are dreaming about.

SAMPLE DREAMS

Hissing Cat

Kim dreamt that she walked into a big empty hall, and out of a dark corner came a cat, hissing at her, hostile, trying to get her to leave. She thought perhaps the cat had had a litter, but that didn't seem to be the case. She wanted to be in this room, when suddenly she realized that she was in the classic position of two cats in a barn. This cat was very jealous of her space and didn't want anybody else in her territory.

When I asked Kim to describe the personality of the cat, she said, "Well, I don't like cats. They're territorial, they're jealous, they're nasty, they scratch, they hiss, they're not warm and generous and open like dogs. I really don't like them." And when I restated that description to her, she said, "You know, that description of a cat describes one of my friends. This friend has a very annoying habit of trying to claim as her territory almost any attractive man we meet when we go dancing together. She looks like a friend—she is a friend in certain ways—but whenever we're around men she becomes just like a hissing cat. There are plenty of men to go around. Just as in the dream, there is plenty of room, but she won't let me into the space. She doesn't want me anywhere near. I've been humoring her, but I think I've really had enough. I have to talk to her about the fact that I'm not willing to play this game anymore."

A Cat Moves In

Tony dreamt that a very furry cat entered the house and planned on staying there. Tony woke up distressed.

Tony described cats as selfish, demanding, very allergenic creatures. He hates cats and was more than a little upset to think of one moving in with him. When he heard the restatement of his description he said, "Oh, no, that sounds like my new girlfriend. I don't like to think that, because she is also very sexy, but she is selfish, she is demanding, and she is very controlling. I think I'd be as allergic to her as I am to cats. I wouldn't be able to breathe in the same space with her."

Starving Kittens

Jan dreamt that she walked out onto the porch of her house in the middle of winter to find several starving kittens in a box. They were hers, but she hadn't realized they were there. They were hungry, neglected, and nearly freezing, and she wanted to cry, she was so sad to see them in this condition.

Jan described kittens as defenseless, playful creatures that need to be well cared for. As she described them she cried, realizing that she felt very much like an abused and neglected little kitten. She had felt that way growing up, and even now as an adult she still felt that inside her were these kittens that needed to be nurtured and cared for. Only now had she discovered the depth of the sadness she had carried with her from a very difficult childhood.

WHAT DO YOU SAY?

1. Pretend I come from another galaxy. What are cats like?
2. Do you like cats? Why or why not?
3. What is the cat in your dream like? What is its personality?
4. Is there anyone in your life or any part of yourself that is like this cat, which you describe as (restate the description)?
5. What is the cat doing in your dream?
6. How does the cat's activity parallel the actions of the person in your life who is like the cat?

Dogs

VARIATIONS

Dreams about dogs are very common indeed. Dogs can be our best friends, our rescuers, or our attackers. Dogs can be generic mutts, or they can appear as very specific breeds or mixtures of breeds. We can dream of healthy or sick dogs, dogs that are limping, dogs that we have to save, dogs that save us. We can see our own dogs from childhood or our friends' dogs. We can see dogs fighting, playing, sleeping.

WHAT OTHERS HAVE SAID

Many of the traditional dream dictionaries say categorically that dogs are symbols of faithfulness. Try telling that to someone who is allergic to dogs or someone whose parent was terribly wounded by a dog. The Jungian Karen Signell writes, "Among its many meanings the dog who guards the door of the house with its alert senses and protectiveness still represents today, as it did in Egyptian times, our loyal companion who guards the threshold to death and helps us across."[2] The Gestalt therapist Frederick Perls spoke of dogs as images of the aggression within the dreamer projected onto a threatening dog. I have found that rabid dogs often represent a part of the dreamer or someone important in the dreamer's life whose aggression and anger are out of control. Many dog dreams have to do with managing dogs well on leashes. These dreams often use the dog to represent a particular quality or personality trait in the dreamer, perhaps something playful, sexual, or rambunctious. Managing the dog on the leash then often represents the dreamer's effort to find the proper level of control over these parts of her or his own personality.

SAMPLE DREAMS

Dog Bite

Lydia dreamt: "I was looking at a picture of my childhood home. There were lots of Joshua trees in the open lot nearby, when suddenly I was no longer looking at a photograph, I was there. I noticed out of the corner of my eye some movement. Suddenly a dog rushed me and bit me on my hand. It seems I was more shocked than hurt. I was shocked because it seemed to be specifically targeting me; this was not a random attack."

Lydia understood this dream to be an unconscious review of some of the important characteristics of her early life. The Joshua trees were among the pretty things of her childhood that she was happy to remember and of which she was rather proud because they were very unusual and elegant compared to the ticky-tacky house in which she grew up. She described the dog as "your basic blended dog" that could be friendly or hostile. In attacking her, the dog was intent upon injuring her. In interviewing Lydia we asked her, "What in your life feels like an attack that is very focused on injuring you, that is like this dog?" She replied, "It's very much like my father's attacks. They would come out of nowhere, and they were very much aimed at hurting me. What is interesting in the dream is that I am not that hurt. I am mostly impressed by the intent of the dog to injure me. My father was sort of a basic dad, and his attacking outbreaks, when I look back on them, are very shocking, although I accepted them as normal as a child. No wonder I have been timid with men. You never know when one is going to turn around and bite you, just as in the dream."

The Sleeping Dog

Sharon dreamt: "A friend and I are hiking on a trail in New Mexico, and we pass a sleeping dog. The dog awakens and snarls at us. I snarl back, and the dog follows me menacingly. When I pick up a rock and threaten him, he retreats. After several things occur in the dream, we are coming back on the trail and the dog is pursuing us again. It is much larger than I thought. I tell my friend, 'We should have grabbed more rocks.' I throw the one I have; it hits the animal, but it doesn't stop it. Now it is not a dog, it's a dark gray hyena with strange square spots of black, white, yellow, and maybe brown. As it comes close to me I see it has red eyes glowing like coals through candied cherries. Its eyes appear watery like it is tired or old or sad. Just as it appears ready to devour us I realize that this animal will not attack; it wants to be friends, it needs me."

In describing the sleeping dog Sharon said it was rather ugly and mean. It reminded her of her husband who snarls a lot, who has a great deal of unresolved anger under the surface, and who stays shut down emotionally. Describing her action of snarling back, Sharon said she was not afraid of the dog, she knows how to handle dogs because her father used to raise them. Next I asked her to describe a hyena, into which the dog had been transformed. She described the hyena as a beautiful animal, a scavenger who eats dead flesh, has a spooky demeanor, is wild and frightening, and is not a respectable carnivore, for it kills its own. She was not happy to tell us that this description also described her husband at his worst. I asked her to describe how she felt about the dog turning into a hyena, and she said she liked the glow under the eyes, she felt sorry for his being sad, and she realized that he needed a friend. She added that her husband was very much like that, although she often forgets about his sadness and his needs because he is so hostile with her. She decided to enter couples' counseling.

WHAT DO YOU SAY?

1. Pretend that I come from another planet and have never heard of a dog. What are dogs like? How do you like dogs in general?

2. What is the dog in your dream like? What sort of personality does this dog have?

3. What is happening with the dog in your dream?

4. Is there anything or anyone or any part of yourself that is like this dog that you describe as (restate the description) and who is acting the same way?

5. How do you cope with the dream dog? Does this parallel any
   situation in your life?

Fish

VARIATIONS

Have you ever dreamt of beautiful fish under water showing off their pearlescent colors and their graceful floating movements? Have you dreamt of stingrays or sharks
threatening you in the water? Some people have even
dreamt of being fish and swimming through the water.
Sometimes fish in dreams are blended images of both a
shark and a seal or a snake and a fish. Fish in dreams may
be healthy or unhealthy. They may be in an aquarium and
being suffocated by not getting enough air or proper care
and treatment. Some fish are hard to see; you just know
they are there somewhere under the murky water. People
feed fish, like koi, by holding pellets of food in their hands
and the koi come and suck out the food. Some dreamers
spend their nights fishing, hoping to catch the big one,
while others find themselves on little boats trying to protect
dolphins from the greedy nets of professional fishermen.
While we are afraid of some fish in dreams, other fish we
adore, value, love, and almost worship.

WHAT OTHERS HAVE SAID

Many people borrow from astrological interpretations of
Pisces in fish and personality styles associated with astrological traditions. Fish are often seen as a symbol of wealth,
of fertility, and of richness, either on a spiritual or physical
plane. One psychoanalyst I know believes that fish are

phallic symbols, although I don't think that belief is very popular among modern psychoanalysts. The French author Raymond De Becker observes that phallic allusions to fish are often made in a superficial manner and that they do not adequately plumb the richness of the symbolic value of the fish. He writes, "The eating of fish signifies the assimilation by the conscious being of a very rich and deep psychic energy."[3]

Many religiously oriented interpreters who are Christian interpret fish in dreams as a symbol of Christ. Jung often saw fish as a symbol of the self, of which Christ could also be an image of the highest, fullest center of being. Signell describes fish as "more remote from conscious knowledge . . . (they represent the movement of life, very primitive or very wise deep down in the water as they were unconscious)."[4] At our dream center, Dr. Flowers and I emphasize that the meaning of any fish in a dream depends entirely upon the specific fish that appears and the particular feelings, attitudes, and associations that the dreamer carries.

SAMPLE DREAMS

The Big One Got Away

Matteo dreamt: "I was fishing off the coast of Sicily and had been out almost all day long. I caught a number of fish, but they were too small and I threw them back. Then I caught a big one. Some friends of mine on the boat distracted me, asking me if I wanted to come have a drink, and the fish got away."

In describing the fish Matteo said, "This fish was huge. It was the one I had been waiting for all day. There were lots of others but they weren't big enough, they weren't right. That makes me think of my search for a wife. I've met a lot of women who are not quite enough for me. Recently I have been going out with a special woman. We are already having some conflict because she is jealous when I go out with my men friends, which I do about three nights a week. I think that maybe my dream is warning me about paying close attention to the relationship if she really is the one I want. I need to pay more attention to her than to my buddies."

Fishy Pool

Taylor dreamt: "I went for a late-night swim in my lover's pool. It was very big and very dark. At first the water was cool and refreshing, but then I began to sense that there were fish swimming below me and I became anxious that they might be poisonous or aggressive fish like sharks or stingrays. I decided to get out of the pool and was quite shaken by the experience."

When Taylor described his lover's pool as cool, refreshing, and inviting, he said his lover was very much like that. She was a woman who was peaceful and calm and cool, and it was very refreshing being with her. When I asked him to describe a stingray, he said they are very graceful fish that float through the water as if they are flying through the air with wings. They look lovely, but they can be extremely poisonous and can attack without warning. When I asked if there was anyone in his life or any part of himself that was like a stingray, he replied that now and then his graceful, peaceful girlfriend would attack without warning. When I asked him what sharks are like, he said that they are the most vicious animals in the sea. Certain species are very aggressive and occasionally will kill a man or bite off his leg when he is just innocently swimming by.

When I asked him if there was anyone in his life or any part of himself that was like a shark, he said that he hated to admit it but his lovely girlfriend did have this occasional habit of attacking out of the blue. In his dream Matteo decided to get out of the water. And eventually he also decided to get out of the relationship. While he was mesmerized by her beauty, calm, and grace, he knew that lurking underneath the calm waters she had some very troubled feelings that would require a great deal of work to resolve.

WHAT DO YOU SAY?

1. What are fish? Pretend I have never heard of them before.
2. What are the fish in your dream like?
3. What are the fish doing in your dream?
4. What are your feelings about the fish in your dream?
5. So you describe the fish in your dream as (restate the description), correct?
6. Is there anything in your life or anyone or any part of yourself that is like the fish in the dream?
7. How so? Test the bridge to make sure the connection is clear and accurate.

Snakes

VARIATIONS

Is there anyone who has never dreamt of snakes? Most often in dreams, a snake is frightening. Snakes may threaten to poison you or to squeeze you to death; sometimes they actually kill the dreamer in the dream. In other cases snakes are the object of adoration and care. People who enjoy having snakes as pets will even dream about snakes as having particular personalities and moods and very specific roles to play within a dream. Some dream snakes are poisonous, while others are harmless. Some are hidden in the grass, and others are on display, as in a zoo.

WHAT OTHERS HAVE SAID

In myths and legends around the world snakes have represented wisdom, rebirth, regeneration, sin and seduction, danger, and sexuality as well as the subtle kundalini energy, or spiritual energy. As usual, fixed interpretations vary widely. In the Talmud snakes were seen as representing richness and wealth, and to kill one in a dream meant to lose all of one's wealth. In China a dream of a snake was seen as foretelling that the next child born would be a daughter, but in India it foretold the death of a son. Artemidorus gave many interpretations, saying that snakes represent an enemy, fertility, and a woman, and to fear a snake suggested that one would become ill. Carl Jung wrote that snakes are "primitive and cold-blooded [and] symbolize the instinctual side of the unconscious." Elsewhere Jung says, "The idea of transformation and renewal by means of a serpent is a well-substantiated archetype. It is the healing serpent representing the god."[5] Signell writes that the snake "with its body close to the earth, with its eyes always open and its venom, is the embodiment of basic earthiness and our fears about unknown powers as well as an ancient symbol of physical and spiritual healing."[6]

For psychoanalysts, of course, the snake is the quintessential phallic symbol. It could symbolize a man's or a woman's desire to have sex or fear of being sexual, or in some cases fear of castration. And let's not forget that for Freud it could always represent penis envy on the part of a female dreamer; I don't think he was joking when he wrote that snakes can be female symbols, since "having no legs, they're totally castrated."[7] Grinstein notes that while a snake could certainly refer to a penis, it could also refer to attributes such as deceptiveness, sneakiness, or trickery or to dangerous qualities in a person in the dreamer's life.

I believe the interpretation of a snake in any given dream depends upon the type of snake, the snake's behavior in the dream, and the dreamer's feelings and reaction to the snake, both in the dream and in waking life.

SAMPLE DREAMS

Snake Fangs

Carla had the following dream: "I walked past a man who was carrying a serpent. It curled around me and attacked me. I could feel its fangs sinking deep into my leg. I was in more shock than pain. I looked at my leg to see the mark of where the bite had been. Was the snake poisonous? My leg was sore. I came to and was told that an acquaintance of mine had just suddenly died for no apparent reason. It made me realize how temporary our existence is. It can all vanish in a moment. My misadventure with a snake wasn't that final. I was alive and I would be all right."

Carla described the snake as being venomous, having a good grip on her, and going deep into her. She saw it as evil and disabling. Carla asked herself, "When have I been attacked by something that's venomous and could sink its fangs into me and also has a good grip on me?" She responded, "I most closely bridge this experience to the mean and malicious attacks from my boyfriend, Clement.

I was surprised when a similar incident happened with my sister over the weekend after the dream, in which I felt my character was attacked. I realized that both my sister and Clement attack because they feel defensive. I have tried to learn not to take this too personally, but the dream seemed to be letting me know that these kinds of encounters are more toxic than I realized. It seems I should stay clear of snake territory."

Eek! A Snake

Beth dreamt: "I screamed as I opened a small box containing some of my jewelry and pens and pencils, because I found a live snake in the box. It was small and thin and probably harmless. I asked who put it in there, and a very pretty, young, sexy acquaintance of mine said she did, and she said that she kept larger snakes among her own things. I wanted her to get rid of them all."

Beth described the snake in her dream as frightening and squirmy, and she didn't like it because she didn't know what it would do next. Although she was afraid of it, she also realized in the dream that it was harmless. She described her young acquaintance as sexy, appealing, and a little mysterious—a person who was not at all afraid of snakes. Beth laughed and said this dream must be about sex. "I grew up in a time when sex was not a topic anyone ever talked about, and I feel uncomfortable dealing with sexuality; I wish it would just go away." The acquaintance in the dream offered her a chance to consider another way of relating to sexuality that might be more fulfilling. Beth also thought that the harmless nature of the snake in her dream referred to her husband who, while sexual, was indeed not going to hurt her.

WHAT DO YOU SAY?

1. What are snakes like? Pretend I've just come from another galaxy and have never seen one before.

2. What is the specific snake in your dream like?

3. How would you describe the personality of the snake in your dream?

4. What is the snake doing in your dream?

5. Is there anyone in your life or anything or any part of yourself that is like this snake, which you describe as (restate the description again)?

6. How so? Be as specific as you can.

Birds

VARIATIONS

We dream of exotic and mundane birds, of crows and pelicans, of cockatiels and peacocks. The birds can be threatening or beckoning. They can soar with great majesty or be imprisoned and needing to be liberated. Sometimes birds will change colors in dreams or change personalities; they may go from being beautiful white creatures of elegance and light to black and threatening birds that bite and attack. Sometimes people dream of shooting down birds, of saving them from oil spills, or of clipping their wings.

WHAT OTHERS HAVE SAID

From ancient times the bird has been the symbol of the soul. In many cultures dreaming of a bird was taken to mean that soon there would be the flight of a soul or the death of someone close to the dreamer. Birds have been associated with liberty, lightness, and freedom. Freud interpreted birds as phallic symbols and said that dreaming of a bird signifies the wish to be sexually competent. Artemidorus taught that big birds in dreams meant wealth and that little birds foretold an improvement in situations for poor people. For some rather silly interpretations we can turn to G. H. Miller, author of a popular dream dictionary, who tells us that "a wealthy and happy partner is near if a woman has dreams of seeing birds with beautiful plumage," or to see a wounded bird "is fateful of deep sorrow caused by erring offspring."[8] Carl Jung described birds as symbols of thought and stated that birds' flight represented the flight of thought; "Generally it is fantasies and intuitive ideas that are represented thus."[9] The Jungian Karen Signell writes that birds "represent what is beyond conscious knowledge: autonomous thoughts that come to us in the form of creative inspirations or spiritual truths. . . . Birds in flight express the elation and excitement of our earliest creative thoughts or spiritual experiences which suddenly and mysteriously appear, but, like birds, as suddenly fly away into the wind and disappear from consciousness, perhaps leaving us as untouched and unenlightened as before the experience."[10] She sees birds as messengers of a new beginning, messengers that promise to guide the dreamer to further development.

SAMPLE DREAMS

A Bird of Passage

Karen dreamt: "I am with friends and colleagues, and we are filming in my living room something green, maybe a forest, a jungle, and a body of water all under the glass. Suddenly a bird that I understand to be a bird of passage rises to the surface, and it dances and twirls for a moment. I say, 'Look! Look how lovely, how graceful it is!' I note as it stops that it is a very sick bird, and it must be put out of the house and take its chances in the wild, probably to die. The bird may well be contagious and a threat to the household. As I put the bird outside the screen door its eyes clearly tell me, 'Oh, please don't put me out, please.' I am heartbreakingly sad, but I must. I linger and I pat it on the head with my right hand. It is glad, even for this small kindness. I awake thinking I need to wash my hand, and I cry."

Karen described the bird in her dream as beautiful, graceful, elegant, but sick and a danger to herself and everyone in her household. She said birds of passage only stay in one place for a short time, and already her interview led her to bridge the bird to her boyfriend who had been living with her. Because he had run out of money, he was causing an extreme financial stress in Karen's life. She felt this dream captured both her appreciation of the charm and grace of her boyfriend as well as her sadness at the idea of putting him out so that he would make it on his own. But the dream went further; it showed her that his essential nature was that of a bird of passage.

The Crow and the Canary

Franklin dreamt: "I was in my childhood bedroom, and I saw a crow enter the room and harass my canary, which I kept in the corner of the room. I was unable, though I tried, to get the crow out of the room."

When I interviewed Franklin, I asked him what canaries are like. He said canaries are beautiful, happy, delicate birds that are used in mine shafts to find out if the air is good enough for humans to breathe. Franklin described crows as very aggressive birds that will try to get the better of any bird in their environment—very territorial and very mean. I asked him if there was anybody or anything in his life like a crow. He said, "My older brother was like a crow, and I was like the canary. I was much more sensitive to the family unhappiness. My brother harassed me all the time." Asked why Franklin would be having this dream now, he said, "One of my co-workers is just like my brother, the crow, and so far I have been unable to shoo him out of my professional life. But at least now I understand why he has such a strong impact on me, since he invokes the same feelings my brother did."

WHAT DO YOU SAY?

1. What are birds like?
2. Describe the bird in your dream. What sort of personality would you say it has? Why do you like or dislike it?
3. What is the bird doing in your dream?
4. Does the bird that you describe as (restate the description) and that is doing (restate the action) remind you of anything, anyone, or any part of yourself?
5. How so? Be as specific as you can in describing the parallels.

Wild Animals

VARIATIONS

Our dreams of wild animals are so often filled with anxiety it's a wonder we can ever sleep through them. In our dreams wild animals might pursue us, corner us, or threaten us. In some cases we might have them on leashes or they might even be friendly, and in rare instances they talk to us. But almost always the dreamer remains poignantly aware of the fact that he or she is in close proximity to an animal that is not tame and must be feared or respected for its wildness. An interesting development in some dreamers' experience is wild animals that get loose from a zoo and perhaps pursue the dreamer, then in later dreams return and come under the control of the dreamer, either by being leashed or befriended. These latter dreams are usually extraordinarily satisfying and pleasurable. They usually signify the dreamer's progress in coping with the people or the aspects of his or her own personality represented by the wild dream animal.

WHAT OTHERS HAVE SAID

In old-fashioned dream analysis, both ancient and recent, many interpreters have formulated and attached specific meanings to a particular animal. Jung interpreted the bear as standing for the dark, threatening, dangerous, or chthonic element of a human being. The contemporary Jungian Karen Signell writes that the bear "represents introverted wisdom and maturity." She adds that the traits of a bear suggest "inner instinctual power and calm introspection."[11] The Freudian Alexander Grinstein notes that dreaded fathers can be represented in dreams as beasts of prey and that "the dreamer's dread of his own wild impulses" can be projected upon the image of the father represented as a wild animal in a dream. Grinstein continues, "At times the wild impulses characteristic of some animals may represent a wished-for freedom to express impulses that are not really wild, but which the individual believes would be considered so by society or by his superego."[12]

At our dream center, Dr. Flowers and I are careful not to suggest possible meanings for wild animals in dreams. Instead, we interview the dreamer and elicit good descriptions of the particular wild animal in a particular dream to find out what the animal means to that dreamer. Sometimes the wild animals follow the interpretations suggested by the psychoanalysts; more rarely they follow Jungians' interpretations. Most of the time, however, wild animals in dreams carry meanings that are specific to the dreamer's own psyche and life. There are an unlimited number of meanings that dreamers may choose to express through their wild dream animals. It's easy to see that a woman who has been attacked at a state park by a grizzly bear in the middle of the night would be unlikely to use a bear in her dream to symbolize maturity and wisdom. More likely, she will use a bear to represent a terrible, powerful threat to her well-being.

SAMPLE DREAMS

Alligator in My Bed

Ari dreamt: "There was an alligator in bed with me. I told myself to remain calm. Then I called 911, and the operator told me to stay calm."

I asked Ari to describe the personality of an alligator. He said they are wild animals that often seem immobile; they move rarely and often slowly, and they usually look very tired. However, when they are on the attack they can move swiftly and kill their prey very easily. I asked him, "What is the personality of an alligator?" He said, "Ambush. They look cool and calm, but they're vicious and they surprise you by suddenly striking fast. They ambush without warning." I asked Ari if there were anyone in his life or any part of himself that was like an alligator. He laughed bitterly and said, "My wife." He is in bed with a wife who looks very placid but can be vicious and attack suddenly. He said that the advice to remain calm from the emergency center seemed appropriate because he had to be careful around his wife or be attacked. He decided to play it very calm to minimize his exposure to her attacks, to make his plans, and then to inform her that he was moving out.

Wild Animal Hospital

Carrie dreamt: "I am working as a volunteer at a wild animal hospital. These animals are orphans, sick, misfits, homeless, or any combination of these things. For example, if someone once had a lion for a pet but did not treat it right and now the lion is a nervous wreck, then it is no good for a zoo. It would come to this hospital."

Carrie described volunteering for these animals as rewarding work. "The animals were very hard to handle and had different needs. Because the work was so difficult, you would be considered very special for working with them since you have done something that has been out of everyone else's control. The animals just are who they are and need to be cared for." Carrie immediately bridged, or connected, these animals to her own conflicted feelings from childhood. They were feelings of being an orphan, of being homeless, of being a misfit, and of being sick. She wrote in her journal, "I matter-of-factly deal with these ferocious animals, dealing with my emotions and feelings. I am very proud that I am volunteering, I want to deal with these wild animals. I am doing a good job."

Later in the dream Carrie dreamt: "When I first come in from my shift at the hospital, I deal with the tiger. He is very mean and ferocious and bites my hand and scratches me. He is very cranky and possibly dangerous. A nurse or doctor in charge takes the young tiger away and explains he has lost his mother and is in a bad mood. The doctors have to deal with him for now."

In describing the dream action Carrie said, "Even though the tiger injures me and I get scared in the dream, still I don't run screaming from the scene. Neither am I paralyzed with fear, as I used to be in other dreams." Carrie described the feelings of the dream tiger as precisely the ones she has felt toward her mother. She wrote, "This is like the fierce anger I have concerning my mother. She never protected me from my abusive father. It's so wonderful to have uncovered that after so many years."

WHAT DO YOU SAY?

1. Describe the wild animal in your dream. What is it like, and what is its personality like?

2. How is a wild animal different from a tame one, and how does this affect the personality of your dream animal?

3. Is there any part of yourself or anyone in your life or anything in your life that is like this wild animal, which you describe as (restate the description)?

4. What is the wild animal up to in your dream? How do you feel about this dream action?

5. Is there anywhere in your life that this dream animal character is acting or feeling as it is in the dream?

6. How so? (Be explicit and be sure you have a good match by comparing the dream action with your life situation.)

Insects

VARIATIONS

Creepy crawlies appear in our dreams. Dream insects are sometimes scary and sometimes overwhelming. Sometimes they are dangerous and poisonous; other times they constitute an out-of-control infestation that makes your skin crawl or even threatens your life. You might dream of a single bee that won't give you any peace. It buzzes around you and threatens you. Or you might dream of a house infested by termites. Yet again, you might dream of a caterpillar and look forward to its evolution into a beautiful butterfly. An entomologist who studies bugs for a career is likely to use specific insects to characterize certain personality traits that he or she associates with a given insect. Meanwhile, people who have an "Eek!" response to insects will be unlikely to use insects in a positive role; more likely, insects in their dreams will express fears and conflicts and difficult people in their lives.

WHAT OTHERS HAVE SAID

Freud wrote that being plagued by vermin is often a sign of pregnancy. Such an interpretation does lead one to wonder what Freud and/or his dreamers felt about pregnancy. Freud also said that according to one of his colleagues, "A spider in dreams is a symbol of the mother, but of the phallic mother, of whom we are afraid; the fear of spiders expresses fear of mother-incest and horror of the female genitals."[13] "The black hairy nature of the spider's body often refers to pubic hair and to the anxieties referable to it. In their association patients will often identify the spider specifically as a black widow spider, a species in which the female destroys the male after intercourse. The dread evoked by this symbol was that the woman, specifically her genitals, will castrate or kill the dreamer, suck the blood out of him, and destroy him just as the black widow spider kills her mate after he has fertilized the eggs and is of no further use to her. Men may have such dreams in connection with impregnation and/or childbirth, thereby expressing the fear that when their biological use has been realized, they will be destroyed by the woman."[14] A child or adult who has seen the animated film *Charlotte's Web* is more likely to dream of a spider as a heroine rather than a bloodsucking mother, don't you think?

The Jungian Karen Signell writes of butterflies, "The butterfly is the universal symbol of natural development and change, symbol of innermost, archetypal transformation, a symbol of the spiritual aspect of life that goes back to prehistoric times."[15] A highly flirtatious female or a womanizing male might dream of a butterfly or honeybee flitting from flower to flower as an image of her or his actions at a particular period in life. The psychoanalysts Fosshage and Loew write, "Insects and other small animals symbolize siblings."[16]

Remember that in your dreams you choose images to use them to your own ends. You express feelings or character traits that you associate with that insect. Beware of accepting any hand-me-downs or fixed meanings. Use other people's ideas to trigger your own ideas and explorations. Form your own verbal description of your dream insect, and consider yourself the highest authority on its meaning.

SAMPLE DREAM

Tarantula

Beatrice dreamt: "I am with Tony. We see what I first call a hairy ape, but is in fact a black, furry tarantula. I note that it flees into a rock and I could kill it there. Tony says that's not good for it. I agree and feel sorry for the tarantula. I don't want to kill or crush it. Then it comes out to the edge, and I realize I've lost my chance to kill it. Now it might bite or poison me."

In her interview Beatrice described a hairy ape as "your typical boyfriend who, like an ape, is more hairy and generally less emotionally developed and refined than a woman." When she looked more closely in her dream she saw that she was dealing with a furry tarantula. In describing tarantulas she said that they hid in dark places, they were secretive, and she wasn't sure but she thought they were potentially poisonous. She was afraid of the one in her dream and wished that in the dream she had killed it when she had the chance. She felt very vulnerable to it.

Beatrice bridged these descriptions to her boyfriend, who, after all, was beside her in the dream. She described Tony as secretive and potentially dangerous to her because he was financially unstable and dependent upon her. Furthermore, the way she felt sorry for the tarantula in the dream perfectly described the way she felt sorry for Tony, who at the moment was unable to make a living. The dream helped her realize that she couldn't afford to spare the tarantula; she had to save herself. She was particularly struck by the fact that what she had first thought to be a relatively harmless ape was indeed a secretive, poisonous tarantula. Blended images like these often show you two aspects of a part of yourself or someone in your life. In cases where, in a dream, you think an animal or insect to be one thing and then discover that it's really another, you are seeing underneath the surface of things with a perceptiveness often unavailable to you while awake.

WHAT DO YOU SAY?

1. Describe the insects in your dream as if you were describing their general nature to someone from another planet. How would you describe the personality of such creatures?
2. How do you like these insects in general?
3. What is the insect in your dream like?
4. What is it up to?
5. How do you feel about the insect in your dream?
6. Is there anything, anyone, or any part of your life that is like the insect you describe?
7. How so?

Turtles

VARIATIONS

Through the years I have been surprised by the number of my clients who dream about turtles. All sorts of dream turtles appear in all sorts of situations. They may be large or small, young or aged, swimming in the sea or in an aquarium, or marching with confidence through a hot, barren terrain. Sometimes the turtles are sick, sometimes happy, and sometimes frightened and withdrawn into their shells.

WHAT OTHERS HAVE SAID

G. H. Miller, author of a popular dream dictionary, interprets turtles in dreams as signifying "that an unusual incident will cause you enjoyment, and improve your business conditions"!

Sigmund Freud said that the roundness of a turtle makes it a female symbol unless it is seen with its arms and legs extended, in which case it could be a male symbol. Or even more Freudian would be an interpretation of the turtle as a symbol of homosexuality, since a turtle can be interpreted (by Freudians) as both male and female.

Carl Jung interpreted a tortoise in this way: "The tortoise is a very impersonal symbol. . . . It has an armored house into which it can withdraw and where it cannot be attacked. . . . It is amphibious, it is apathetic, it lives a very long time, and it is highly mythological and mysterious."[17] Emphasizing the turtle's mythological dimension of wisdom and great age, he concludes that the tortoise is a symbol of the union of opposites, the transcendent function. The Swiss existentialist Medard Boss interpreted a turtle as expressing the dreamer's view of her animal side as "a cold-blooded armored creature, remote from human modes of existence."[18]

Usually interpretations of a dream symbol as male or female are based on ideologies that are fairly rigid and dated in their conceptions of men and women. Furthermore, calling something a male or female symbol yields such a vague interpretation that it rarely adds much to a practical, useful understanding of the dream. However, if considering images as masculine or feminine originates with the dreamer, then any interpretation that springs from this type of description will be meaningful according to the dreamer's belief system.

Let's look at two of my clients' dreams.

SAMPLE DREAMS

Turtle Sushi

Carmen dreamt: "I am sitting in a restaurant and see that the waiter has just placed our main course in a serving dish on the center of the table. Our main course is turtle sushi. A turtle on its back is all cut up for us to eat. I burst into tears and awake."

When I asked Susana to describe a turtle to me as if I had never seen such a thing before, she said, "Turtles are very tough on the outside but very vulnerable on the underside. They are self-sufficient and even-paced." To the question "What is the turtle in your dream like?" she responded, "He was helpless, flipped on his back, and his tender underside was all sliced up to be consumed by us." When I asked her if this description reminded her of anyone, anything, or any part of herself, she burst out, "Yes! That is my father. He is very old and very hard, but the dream makes me see for the first time how vulnerable he is in his old age. His heart really is tender under his shell, but we, his children, are sort of carving him up waiting to divide his estate when he dies. I have been so angry at him, I've forgotten my love for his tender underside!"

While certain commonly noted characteristics of turtles played a part in Susana's dream, you can see that the particular mix of characteristics shown in the context of her dream and her feelings both about turtles and about the particular turtle in her dream were vital to a clear, specific, useful interpretation.

Slow Turtle

Howard, a hardworking surgeon, dreamt of hooking a big fish while standing at a turbulent seaside. The strike was too big for the tackle. As the line neared its end, he noticed that it was frayed and that if it kept going out it would break. He began to run along the beach in the direction of his prey to take the tension off the line. He reached a tranquil, pleasant beach area and suddenly gained control of the line. He pulled in the catch, which to his surprise was a big turtle. Howard awoke and recognized that he was overworked and indeed reaching the end of his line.

When asked what turtles are and what they are like, Howard said, "Why, they are just friendly, peaceful little critters. They know how to live; they just carry their house around with them and spend their days basking in the sun. They are such slow-moving things!" He described his dream turtle as very big, slow moving, and unperturbed at being brought onto the shore. Howard immediately connected the image to his own frayed edges and concluded that he should slow down. He was struck by the wisdom of the turtle's attitude toward life. He took a vacation to tend to his frayed edges and to look again at his tendency to overwork.

WHAT DO YOU SAY?

To discover the personal meaning of your dreams about turtles, ask yourself these questions. You can use these questions to interpret any animal figure in your other dreams; just substitute your animal for the word *turtle*.

1. What are turtles like? Pretend that I come from another planet and have never heard of turtles before. (Remember, we need to know what you think about turtles, not what I think.) Make your

description brief, with three or four adjectives to describe what you think and feel about turtles.

2. How would you describe the personality of a turtle?

3. What is the turtle doing in your dream?

4. So this turtle is (restate the description, using the same words and tone), right? Feel free to modify or clarify your description so that it accurately reflects your thoughts and feelings about turtles in general and especially about the turtle in your dream.

5. Is there anyone in your life, anything, or any part of yourself that is like this turtle, which you describe as (restate the description)? (By repeating your descriptive words as you look for the metaphoric connection or "bridge" to your real life, you will be supplying yourself with the triggers for more accurate and personal interpretations.)

6. How so? (Here you can test the strength of your bridge or connection. Make sure that your description of your turtle really does match the person, part of yourself, or thing you bridged it to. Don't settle for an easy answer or too vague a one. If you find that the bridge is not a good one, go back to the first three description questions and see if you can make a richer description that will make the connection or interpretation more obvious to you.)

5 Objects in Dreams

How to Interpret Any Object in Your Dreams

The following dream interview questions will be very useful to you as you try to figure out the meaning of any object in your dream. If you dream of a blended object, one that seems to be both this and that, describe each object in turn and then ask yourself to describe the blended object. For example, if you dream of a motorbike that is both motorbike and wheelchair, describe first a motorbike and then a wheelchair, and then see what the blended object would be like.

Don't forget to keep in mind that the interviewer comes from another planet and wants a straight, simple answer that includes the facts as well as your feelings about the particular image.

1. What is this object like? Pretend I come from Mars.

2. Why do humans have or use these objects, and how do they work?

3. How do you feel about these objects generally?

4. What is the object in your dream like?

5. How do you feel about the object in your dream?

Malfunctioning Cars

VARIATIONS

Car dreams are so common that although we have discussed cars in general and dreams in which someone else is driving in the section called "Dream Themes," we have yet to discuss the memorable dreams of malfunctioning cars. Typically, in this kind of dream we are in cars that break down or have no brakes, or we can't figure out how to use the brakes. The car may belong to us or to someone in the family, often a spouse or boyfriend or girlfriend. Sometimes we consult mechanics to help us repair the cars—the mechanics may or may not be helpful—and sometimes we just try to fix the cars on our own with varying degrees of success.

WHAT OTHERS HAVE SAID

Anne Faraday, author of *The Dream Game,* and most modern dream analysts look at cars in which the driver has difficulty controlling the car as expressions of the dreamer's difficulty in controlling his or her own impulses or drives in life. When a car is broken down, most analysts want to know whose car broke down, and they ask questions to find out if the car might represent a co-worker or perhaps the dreamer's psychological well-being or physical health. When a car is broken down, I think it's very important to ask whose car is in trouble and whose responsibility it is to maintain and repair it.

While Freudians often interpret difficulty in getting the car started or keeping it from stalling or engaging the clutch as a male dreamer's concern about his sexual potency, there are many more possibilities. They include, but are not limited to, using the theme of a car that you can't get started as a metaphor for having trouble getting your career started or getting your life started. Can you get your car into gear, can you get yourself into gear? Difficulty in engaging the clutch could also symbolize difficulty in engaging your own energies to be able to get going in a career or in a relationship. Slashed tires on your car could symbolize your feeling of being slashed by difficult circumstances in life or by friends, colleagues, or enemies.

SAMPLE DREAMS

Let My Wife Fix the Car

Vincent dreamt: "I've gone on vacation with my wife. The car is broken down. It's my job to get it fixed. This was the beginning of a long dream but it certainly set the tone."

Asked what in his life was like the broken-down car, Vincent was quick to bridge the car to his marriage. He said that his marriage to Justine was certainly broken down and that he had taken the responsibility to fix it since she was not interested in helping. As you might imagine, the rest of the dream did not go very well for Vincent, who throughout the dream was being overly responsible and was not getting the support or assistance that he needed to repair his marriage. The dream highlighted his tendency to take responsibility and his wife's tendency to sit back and let him do all the work. In a later dream he took the car in to a mechanic who was a representation of the couples' counselor they were seeing. Even with the mechanic's help, Vincent was unable to repair the car to its original state. It was time for Vincent to realize his limitations, that his wife needed to get to work if she wanted to save the marriage.

Personality Car

Alissa dreamt: "I was driving a wonderful sports car. I was having so much fun. It was exhilarating, thrilling, and I felt strong and delirious to be alive. Then I realized the brakes didn't work, and I started trying to figure out how I would stop the car without crashing."

I asked Alissa to describe the car. She said it was a lovely, fun, red car. I asked her what the personality was of such a car. She described it as racy, playful, and capable of high-performance achievements. I asked her if there was anything in her life that felt like this car, and she said, "Oh, yes. My new career. It's racy. High performance is very important. I'm really good at it, and it's very snazzy, like the car." I asked her if there was any way she had trouble putting the brakes on in her career. She replied that she did have trouble there. She was hoping the career wouldn't cause her too much difficulty in the future because right now she was so excited, traveling all over the world, achieving things she never thought she would achieve. I asked her to pretend I came from another planet and to tell me what is wrong with not having brakes in such a car. "It would be a disaster; that one joy ride would be your last. Without good brakes such a car would be a death machine." She looked at me and said, "My husband has called my career a death machine. I'm going to have to figure out something. I don't want to give up my husband, I don't want to give up my life, and I don't want to give up my career." This was the first time Alissa had taken a serious look at the aspect of her career that threatened the rest of her life.

WHAT DO YOU SAY?

1. Describe the car in your dream. What is the personality of such a car?

2. Describe what is malfunctioning in the car and why it is a problem. Pretend you are speaking to an interviewer who comes from another planet, and be very concrete and specific.

3. Whose car is in the dream?

4. Does your description of the car and its malfunctioning describe the person who owns the car, some part of yourself, or some situation such as your marriage or your career?

5. How important is this malfunctioning problem?

6. Does the malfunctioning in the car match any malfunctioning area of your life?

7. Is there anything you can do to repair or rectify the situation, and are you sure it is your responsibility to do it?

Chocolate Sauce and Other Foods

VARIATIONS

We dream about food surprisingly often. The food may be abundant and delicious or it may be scarce and spoiled. We may have trouble finding the food we are looking for, or we may be disappointed to find that the promised food was not delivered. It is important to know whether the dreamer considers the food to be healthy or unhealthy. Sometimes organizations provide or withhold food, sometimes intimates of the dreamer play this role, and sometimes the dreamer frets because she has forgotten to provide certain foods to an honored guest or a beloved intimate.

WHAT OTHERS HAVE SAID

The conservative psychoanalysts James Fosshage and Clemens Loew consider eating to be frequently a symbol of coitus. Wine sometimes represents genital secretions, so that, for instance, a husband who spills wine at the table would be told that this dream symbolized his sexual excitement and ejaculation and his wife's vagina, while the table could be a symbol of bed and intercourse.

I must say, I have never heard a dreamer arrive at such conclusions on his own. I think that dreams of foods, while they may have sexual interpretations, can serve many other purposes as well. If the food is healthy, many modern and New Age analysts will interpret it as representing soul food or food that helps to nourish the well-being—psychological, spiritual, as well as physical—of the dreamer. The action and dramatic plot of the dream will determine more specific meanings. If the dreamer is starving for a certain food and is unable to find it, he or she, by describing the food as if describing it to someone from another planet, can usually figure out that the food represents some way of feeling or some form of attention that the dreamer longs for. If the food in your dream is poisoned, it's terribly important to find out who has poisoned the food and ask yourself where in your life you are looking for nurturing or sustenance but finding only poisoned food. It may be an institution or someone in your life, such as a parent or spouse, who is poisoning love through their criticism, control, and other destructive behaviors and attitudes. People who eat too much or too little often have dreams of eating good foods or foods that are bad for them, of dieting, or of overeating. These images usually help the dreamer to see a little more deeply how his or her behaviors around food are symptoms of deeper feelings of discontent or conflict.

SAMPLE DREAMS

No Chocolate Sauce

Bridget dreamt a version of a dream I have heard often: "I am at my wedding (which will not occur for another six months), and I am sitting down to the dessert I had so longed for, but I realize there is no chocolate sauce. I am so disappointed! And I am angry! I turn to my groom and scream, 'There's no chocolate sauce here!'"

The dream interviewer in our group said to Bridget, "Pretend I come from another planet and have never heard of chocolate sauce. What is it?" Bridget smiled and said, "Oh, it's warm and sweet and delicious. It's a topping that goes on the best things in life. In fact, I can't imagine having a life without chocolate sauce." The interviewer asked, "Is there anything about your relationship that makes you think you have to live a life without chocolate sauce?" Bridget said, "Well, when I think of it in the context of my fiancé, I think chocolate sauce for me represents very sensual, luscious, delicious sexuality. I am worried that my husband, who is not very inspiring in this area, might never develop into a good lover. I guess I had better talk to him about it more directly, because it really is important to me. I'm not going to live a life without chocolate sauce."

Forgotten Entrée

Warren dreamt: "I have invited my girlfriend to dinner. I've done a nice job, and I serve her the food, but at the end of the dinner I realize that I forgot the main course. I hope she won't notice."

I asked Warren to pretend I come from another planet and to tell me what a main course is and why humans eat them. He said that it's the most important part of the meal; it might not be the flashiest part, but it's the basic protein and it's the part that most people think that you should never do without. I asked if there was anywhere in his life where he feels he has forgotten the main course, the part one should never do without, particularly in his relationship with his girlfriend. He had no trouble bridging to the fact that he had a friendly, easy relationship with his girlfriend but that he did not love her. He said she loved him, but he just didn't and couldn't serve her the main course. He hadn't been up front about this because he was hoping the relationship could last for a while since it was a very pleasant one even if it wasn't going to be for him the real thing. The dream made him realize that he was asking a lot to hope that she wouldn't notice that he hadn't come through with the main course.

My Mother, the Tomato

Patti had the following dream: "I am in a place something like a museum where things are on display and meant to be studied. On a pedestal is a dish with liquid in it and what appears to be a peeled, canned tomato. It has two eyes on the top, like a sea creature, and it moves around on the plate. It is very sensitive. I try to touch it, and it scuttles away to the other side of the bowl. It is my mother! I am aware this is where I came from. This is my mother."

Patti understood in this dream that the tomato symbolized her mother, but we wanted to know why in the world she would use a tomato. So we asked her to describe tomatoes. She said that they are very soft: "This one is skinless, it's very soft, it's fleshy, you can see its veins, it seems suspicious and self-protective. That really does describe my mother. It also describes how, whenever I tried to touch her, she'd have to scuttle away."

This object was just the first part of a long, complicated dream that helped Patti understand the role that her mother and her relationship with her mother played in Patti's sexual and relational life. Seeing her mother as a tomato that was sometimes inside Patti in a later part of the dream helped her understand some of her own feelings of vulnerability and where they came from.

WHAT DO YOU SAY?

1. Describe the food in your dream as if you were describing it to someone from another planet. Why do you like or dislike it?

2. How does eating this food make you feel?

3. What is the context for the food in your dream? Is it being withheld or poisoned or offered abundantly?

4. Are there any other people in your dream, such as a server or withholder of the food or someone with whom you share it?

5. Describe (using the questions in the section of this book called "People in Dreams") each of the major people in your dream.

6. Is there any situation in your life that matches the description of the food in the context of your dream?

7. How do you feel about this situation, and is there anything you'd like to do about it?

Drugs (Including Cigarettes and Alcohol)

VARIATIONS

We sooner or later dream about substances that we use inappropriately. Smokers dream of cigarettes, alcoholics of alcohol, and drug users of drugs. People who live with those who abuse these substances also tend to dream about the substances. The dreams can show craving and falling off the wagon, where you suddenly partake of something you have given up, or, in very lucky circumstances, the dream may motivate the dreamer to give up the habit once and for all or may encourage the dreamer to start working on getting its use under control. Frequently the emotional color and the action of the dream describe in metaphoric terms the emotional habits that lead one to maintain a destructive habit. These dreams can also be warnings that the dreamer is getting involved in circumstances or in relationships that could lead to falling off the wagon once again. Less frequently, people who do not have a particular problem with a substance will dream of it as a metaphor for unhealthy ways of relating to others or to oneself.

WHAT OTHERS HAVE SAID

Doctors Loma Flowers and Joan Zweben[1] have recently conducted a very interesting study going beyond the traditional psychoanalytic assumption that substance-use dreams are wish-fulfillment dreams. While they agree with the psychoanalysts that, especially in the stages of early recovery, these dreams can be literal, they and Dr. Harry Fiss[2] point out that the feelings a dreamer has upon waking from substance-use dreams indicate the success the dreamer will have in recovering from his or her addiction. People who awake from a using dream feeling disappointed that they didn't have a hit of the drug or a drink of the alcohol are less likely to be committed to their recovery than are those who wake from such a dream relieved that they didn't fall off the wagon last night, that it was just a dream.

SAMPLE DREAM

Smoking Some Grass

Dottie dreamt: "I was at a party, and there were lots of fun people around, but all I could think of was going into a back room and smoking some grass. As I went to the back of the house I was sorry that I would be missing the party."

I asked, "Dottie, what is grass, and why do humans smoke it?" She said, "It's a fairly harmless substance that is overly regulated by the government. It helps you to relax and makes you feel content with the world." I asked her how she felt about going to the back room. She said she regretted that she felt compelled to smoke because "really, I would have had more fun being straight and staying at the party with my friends." I asked her if there was anything in her life that was like grass, that made her feel good and relaxed but at the same time pulled her away from being with her friends in a partylike straight environment. She said her boyfriend was like that; she withdrew from a lot of her friends to be with her boyfriend who indeed made her feel wonderful and who was sexy and very attentive to her. But she also thought she had given up a lot of her life to be with him since he was not very gregarious. Then she looked surprised and said, "You know, I use him as a drug, as a security blanket to avoid challenging and threatening situations, because I feel so safe with him."

WHAT DO YOU SAY?

1. Describe the drug in your dream as if you were describing it to someone from another planet. Why do humans use it?

2. If you use it, why do you, and how does it make you feel?

3. Describe the dream context in which this drug appears.

4. Is there any way in your life that there is something like this drug or the drug itself which plays a role in your life as it does in the dream?

5. How do you feel about the drug in your dream?

6. How do you feel about it when you are awake? If the drug seems more dangerous to you while dreaming than while awake, consider the possibility that you are at greater risk for damaging yourself or your life by using this drug than you may realize.

7. How do you feel when you awake from a dream in which you are using the drug? Do you awaken relieved that it was only a dream and you aren't actually using it, or do you awaken disappointed that it wasn't the real thing and crave it during the day?

Clothes

VARIATIONS

Have you ever dreamt of being in a different time and place where people were dressed in, say, Victorian clothes or Roman togas? Perhaps clothing has been an important image in your dreams in more specific ways. Have you ever forgotten your overcoat or had your jacket stolen? Perhaps you've dreamt of particularly interesting shoes or of wearing shoes that were not yours or didn't fit. Many women have dreamt of wedding dresses and veils, some of which were forced on them by their mothers, others that fit poorly, others that fit like a dream. Perhaps you have dreamt of looking in the mirror and seeing yourself dressed in an unusual fashion, such as a beautiful red dress you would never normally have the courage to wear, or noticing that you were wearing your sister's clothing, which really didn't become you at all. Many of us have dreamt of being barefoot in a dream, to our great delight or to our inconvenience, discomfort, or anxiety.

WHAT OTHERS HAVE SAID

Jung sometimes described clothing as the uniform one wears or the outer personality one shows to the world. He noted, as do many contemporary analysts, that clothing also protects one from the outside world.

SAMPLE DREAMS

If the Shoes Don't Fit

Veronica had the following dream: "I am getting dressed for my wedding but the wedding dress doesn't look right; it doesn't fit me properly. My mother keeps coming up to me and giving me shoes, and I keep giving them back to her saying, 'Mother, they don't fit, they don't fit.' Every pair of shoes she came with was the wrong size."

When I asked Veronica what it was like to be in a wedding dress that didn't fit she said, "Well, it wasn't bad, but it wasn't right either, it just didn't feel comfortable. Some parts were too tight, some parts were too loose." I asked, "Is there anything in your life that doesn't fit, like your wedding dress, too loose here, too tight there?" She said,

"Sometimes I think my fiancé doesn't fit me quite right, but then nobody is perfect and nothing is totally easy, so I don't know if I should let that bother me." I asked her about the shoes that didn't fit and about her mother's insistence that she try one pair after the other. She said that reminded her of her mother's encouragement to marry. She felt a lot of pressure from her to get married, even if the fit wasn't right. She understood her dream: if the shoe fits, wear it; if it doesn't, don't.

Barefoot in the Parade

Kristin, in her late twenties, dreamt: "I was taking a midday break from school, and I noticed a wonderful parade coming by. I wanted to go up and see the parade, but I noticed I was enjoying the warm sun in my bare feet. That part was nice, except that now without any shoes on I had to walk very slowly and very carefully to make sure I didn't hurt my feet on glass and other debris in the street. I had to get through the crowd to see the parade. I really wanted to see it, but I didn't think I'd get there in time because I had to take such care in walking."

I asked Kristin, "Why do humans go barefoot?" She said, "To enjoy the freedom and the wonderful feelings of sand." I asked, "How does it work to be barefoot in your dream?" She said it was a problem because it made her feet vulnerable to injury. When I asked what shoes were for, she said, "In this case, shoes would be to protect my feet so I could walk wherever I wanted to. This parade was like the parade of life." I asked, "Is there any way that you're not able to join or take a look at the parade of life because your feet are unprotected and your feet are vulnerable to injury?" She said yes, in fact this past year of her life she had been taking a break from regular work and schooling to explore her feelings. She said that her psychotherapy had been so intense that she felt extremely vulnerable. "I feel that I am much more focused on my feelings and am turned inward too far, although, like feeling the warmth of the sun, I love feeling my deeper emotions."

Kristin said that the parade was a metaphor for the excitement of life. Her missing dream shoes were helping her reflect upon the level of introversion that would allow her to move out into the parade of life.

WHAT DO YOU SAY?

1. Describe the article of clothing in your dream. First give a generic description. For example, what is a shoe or a glove or an overcoat? Why do humans wear such things, and how do you like them?

2. What is the article of clothing in your dream like?

3. Do you or would you wear such a thing? Why or why not?

4. So, you say this (article of clothing) is (restate the description), and your opinion of it is (restate your feelings about it). Anything you would like to add or modify?

5. What is happening regarding the piece of clothing? Are you looking for it, wearing it, showing it off, or what?

6. How do you feel in the dream regarding the article? Are you proud or puzzled, or are you feeling ashamed or embarrassed by it or by its absence?

7. Is there anything in your life that is like this piece of clothing? Or anything that makes you feel like you are wearing (or have lost or are not wearing) this article of clothing?

Trees

VARIATIONS

Trees in dreams can be spectacular or mundane. In some dreams a tree is healthy and vibrant and exudes a sense of aliveness and growth. In other dreams a tree is withered, dry, sick, or threatened with destruction by an ax or a bulldozer. Trees can evoke strong feelings in dreams—feelings of love and attachment, of loss, of fidelity. A dreamer may dream of a specific kind of tree, which will carry very particular meanings for that person, or the well-being of whole forests can be the central concern of a dream.

WHAT OTHERS HAVE SAID

In most cultures trees have represented abundance and fertility, often happiness, and often life itself. The health of a tree has often been said to mirror the mental or the psychological health of the dreamer or of people in the dreamer's life that the tree brings to mind. Trees have been seen as phallic symbols and the cutting of trees as a fear of castration or a wish to castrate the father. Jungians have interpreted trees more often as symbols of the self, of the potential growth and rootedness of the dreamer in the world. At our dream center we have seen many particular meanings determined by the specific kind of tree and its state of well-being as well as its role in the dream. Raymond De Becker, a French author, notes that trees can serve as an intermediary between heaven and hell, between our highest aspirations and our deepest roots.

SAMPLE DREAMS

Sturdy Pines

Allessandra dreamt: "I look out over my favorite park and see that someone has cut down all the pretty flowering trees. Only the sturdy pines are left standing."

Allessandra described the trees that had been cut down as beautiful, blossoming, graceful trees that added great joy to her world and to her appreciation of the park in which she regularly strolled. When asked, "Is there anything in your life that is like these trees, which you describe as blossoming and graceful?" she could think of nothing. When asked, "Is there any way that you feel some graceful part of your life has been cut down?" she started to cry and said, "Yes, I've been a lawyer now for ten years, and when I look at my life, all that's left are the sturdy pines; in other words, the part of my life that is sturdy, strong, and stable, that is green all year round, and that never changes. That's my professional self. But the part of me that likes to play and be feminine and joyous—I've cut it down myself. I've removed that part of my life until all I have left is my professional self. I don't spend much time with my friends, I don't have time for romance, and I guess the park in my life is a rather boring one."

The Grafted Tree

At the end of a rather long dream William dreamt of sitting down to talk with his father. "Next, I am across the street in the old park near my family home, sitting with someone. I notice a small bristlecone pine tree growing beside the old, dry lawn. Looking more carefully, I see that it is growing inextricably with an old oak. Neither is in very good condition. Both have old, broken branches and have lost some foliage. Looking at their trunks, though, I see they are inextricably grafted together. The bark of the bristlecone in some places is effectively the bark of the oak."

William described the bristlecone pine as an ancient tree that lives in very adverse conditions. With very little water, it can live in the wind and the cold. When I asked him if there were any part of himself, any part of his life, or anyone in his life who was like this ancient tree that lived under adverse conditions with little water, in the cold and wind, he immediately said, "I do, and that's how my life has felt lately." I asked him to describe the old oak in the dream, and he said oaks are grand old deciduous trees in California. They are very strong, they need richer soil than the bristlecone pine and not too much water, and they are very intricate in shape. "That reminds me of my wife," William said. "She is very much a California person, she doesn't need much water, and her soul doesn't want too much." I asked William what was happening with these two trees, and he replied that they are grafted together. When I asked, "Is that normal for trees on earth, or is that a problem?" he explained it is very unhealthy because neither tree is doing well. "One uses up the energies of the other, and it would be very important to figure out how to separate them without killing both, because they are fused together." This reminded William of the last decade of his marriage, with William and his wife so enmeshed and fused with each other that neither had enough of a separate life to feel like an individual. William felt that in the dream he was learning something from sitting down and talking with his father. William felt the fused trees depicted not only his own relationship but also the kind of relationship his mother and father had had.

WHAT DO YOU SAY?

1. What is a tree? Pretend I come from another planet and have never heard of a tree before. How do you feel about trees generally?

2. What is the tree in your dream like? Can you describe its personality?

3. How do you feel about the tree in your dream?

4. Let me see if I've got this right. A tree is (restate the description), right?

5. Does the tree in your dream, which you describe as (restate the description), remind you of any part of yourself or of anyone or anything in your life?

6. How so? Test the bridge, or connection, between the dream image and your waking life.

PART 3

Getting Really Good at Working with Dreams

6 Becoming Your Own Dream Expert

Create a Program of Learning and Practice

For the rest of your life, every single night you will create and experience dreams that deal with every important issues that concern you. These dreams will constitute some of the most honest, creative, and insightful thinking and feeling you will ever do. Take advantage of your dreams. Spend a little time now learning to interpret them, and enjoy the fruits of your interpretive skills for the rest of your life.

There are four main avenues to dream expertise. All are fascinating. You can learn from a good dream analyst, you can work with a dream partner, you can join or organize a dream study group, and you can use books, workbooks, and video- and audiocassettes to develop your skills. Here are a few suggestions that should help you create a program tailored to your needs and interests.

Tools for Solo and Group Dream Study

I've been working for years to create tools that will enable people to understand their own dreams. Here they are:

The Dream Kit (HarperSanFrancisco, 1995): This tool kit includes a workbook that shows you how to recognize patterns in your dreams and provides nightly, weekly, monthly, and yearly review sheets. It also includes instructions for incubating or targeting your dreams for specific problem solving (how to "sleep on it"). There is an audiocassette on how to work with your dreams and how to put yourself to sleep listening to the last ten minutes of the tape.

The best part of the kit is a pack of cue cards that you can hold in your hands as you work with your own or a partner's dream. These cards cue you to ask appropriate interview questions at the right time, and they greatly speed your learning. We use the cards in my study groups and at large workshops and lectures with great success.

Living Your Dreams (HarperCollins, 1996): This book shows you how to target your dreams on a given night to help you understand and solve a practical, emotional, or creative problem. It provides many ideas for putting your dreams to work to improve your problem-assessment and problem-solving skills in many areas of your personal and professional life. I first wrote this in 1977, and since then the book has been used in business schools and training programs around the country and in Europe, India, and Asia to teach people how to tap their nocturnal problem-solving abilities. This is a good introduction to dream interpretation and a classic in the use of dreams for practical problem solving.

Breakthrough Dreaming (book) (Bantam, 1991): A thorough, step-by-step manual for people interested in becoming really good dream interviewers. Very helpful for people working on their own. Includes instructions on conducting dream groups and an extensive bibliography with commentary. This is my favorite book.

Breakthrough Dreaming (two audiocassette programs): Five tapes and a workbook on dream incubation and interviewing with a little history of dreaming thrown in. Great for spouses who think dreams are silly. Mail order via Nightingale Conant, 1–800–323–5552.

Simon and Schuster has produced a two-tape version of *Breakthrough Dreaming* (1996), which is available in bookstores. If you have friends who do not understand or appreciate your interest in dreaming, you can usually get them to react less superficially and think more deeply by having them listen to a few tapes.

Sensual Dreaming: How to Understand and Interpret the Erotic Content of Your Dreams (Fawcette, 1994): Well, don't you think it's about time we take a contemporary look at what our sexual dreams are all about? These can be powerfully liberating dreams that help us understand our sexual inhibitions, conflicts, and in some cases wounds. Men love this book. If you have a boyfriend you would like to interest in dreaming and in opening up his heart, this may be a temptation he won't turn down.

New Directions in Dream Interpretation (State University of New York Press, 1991): This book presents eight approaches to dream interpretation with chapters written by the colleagues I most admire. Bookstores will special order it if you insist, or you can call 1–800–666–2211.

Bring Me a Dream (videocassette): Dr. Flowers and I discuss and demonstrate the use of dreams for specific

278 ● Getting Really Good at Working with Dreams

problem solving with four students. To order, Call the Delaney & Flowers Dream Center at 1–415–587–3424.

The Delaney & Flowers Dream Center

Dr. Loma Flowers and I began in 1981 offering classes and programs to professionals and amateurs who want to develop their dream skills. We have programs for local and out-of-town students at all levels of expertise, and we offer a diploma program as well. We conduct individual, pair, and group classes throughout the year. We work with some students by phone, and we teach around the country and in Europe whenever we can. Send a double-stamped, self-addressed envelope to the Delaney & Flowers Dream Center, 337 Spruce St., San Francisco, CA 94118, or call us at 1–415–587–3424.

How to Choose a Good Dream Analyst

Working individually with a skilled dream analyst can be one of the fastest and most rewarding ways to learn your dream language. This is an expensive approach, and there are several alternatives, including working with the analyst in pair, group, and class settings. A word of warning: a number of practicing dream teachers have little experience or skill. Some are also so authoritarian that you might feel worked over after a session. To find a competent dream analyst, you might read two or three books on dreaming and choose an approach that makes sense to you. Then contact the authors you like and ask for referrals to people in your area who teach dream skills. Here are some questions you might ask a prospective dream analyst.

1. What education and training in dream work have you had?

2. What is your approach to dream interpretation?

3. What are your three favorite books on dreaming? (Then take a look at them.)

4. How long have you been working with dreamers and in what contexts? (Some analysts have had little or no experience working with actual, real-life dreamers, and their approach may have much to do with theory and little to do with the issues of real life.)

5. Over what length of time do you usually work with a client? (It's helpful to have an analyst who sees the fruits of her or his work over time. This increases your chances of finding someone who gets results. Some analysts work only over weekend workshops, and they can never know if they are doing a good job or not.)

Remember that you are the client who hires someone to teach you how to do this for yourself. Don't get mesmerized and stuck with someone who plays the holier-than-thou guru or the wiser-than-thou therapist. Dreams offer you direct access to your own powers of insight. Don't hand these powers over to anyone.

Finding a Dream Partner

Whether you work with a dream analyst or not, finding a dream partner will be one of the most effective things you can do to gain expertise in dream work. By playing the role of the interviewer for another person, you will learn how to ask the right questions at the right time much more quickly than you will when working alone. It's a riveting experience to work with someone's dreams, and it teaches you skills you will use on your self, your toughest client!

To find a partner, consider planning to work for at least one hour a week together. You can meet in person or over the telephone. The phone is a great medium for dream work; I have clients who live all over the country and the world with whom I have regular phone sessions, and it works very well. Even with nearby clients whose schedules are tight, a phone meeting cuts out the commute time. When you work with a dream partner, sometimes even if you are neighbors, the phone is more convenient, and you can have your sessions while you are tucked into bed!

Remember that working with dreams will bring out very personal material, so be sure you choose a partner you trust and respect. Keep strict confidentiality, and try to be reliable in keeping your appointments with each other. This will keep you both motivated. The most precious benefit you will gain from working with a partner is a kind of friendship that will knock your socks off—open, courageous, supportive, instructive, challenging, and, in time, incredibly sweet and strong.

If you don't have a potential dream partner among your friends, meet other dreamers at dream lectures, courses, workshops, and dream study groups. You might join the Association for the Study of Dreams (703–242–8888). Check out our newsletter and the journal *Dreaming*. Come to our conferences and meet hundreds of dreamers from all over the States and the world. Presentations range from experiential workshops to lectures by therapists, researchers, authors, artists, and people from the most diverse fields who have a keen interest in dreaming.

How to Join or Organize a Dream Group

If you are fortunate enough to work in a good dream group for at least six months, you will learn much about dreams, about how to listen and how to relate without intrusion and control, and about human nature. Hearing people tell their dreams over time shows you their real insides. People who are intent upon understanding their dreams are wonderful to watch and to know. They work at being open and honest. For this they have to be courageous and—that most appealing attribute—emotionally curious. To see someone. bravely go after the meaning of his own or another's dream puzzle is a privilege and a fascinating pleasure.

Check with your favorite authors to see if they offer groups or know of some near you. Through the Delaney & Flowers Dream Center, Loma Flowers, M.D., and I lead weekly and monthly groups in and around San Francisco. We also offer Brief Intensive study programs for people who travel to work with us for a few days to several months at a time. Call 415–587–3424 for more information, or write us at the address listed above for the Dream Center. My esteemed and beloved colleague, Dr. Erik Craig, leads study programs in Santa Fe through the Santa Fe Center for the Study of Dreams. You can call Erik at 505–986–8666.

You may not find a group near you, so why not start one yourself? You do not need to be an expert. As a rank beginner, you can render a great service to others looking for a group by providing a forum for you all to learn together. You organize the four to six people, provide a meeting spot, and suggest good reading. I wrote my book *Break-through Dreaming* as a handbook for people who want to learn the Dream Interview method. Groups read one chapter every week and discuss the material at each meeting. The book includes a chapter on conducting group sessions.

Here are a few pointers for organizing a dream group:

1. Choose four to six people who can be trusted to keep confidentiality, to attend regularly, and to make an honest effort to listen, practice, and learn. If you avoid people who talk too much and who need to control others, your group will run much better.

2. If you are a beginner, present yourself as an organizer, not an expert. Take the pressure off yourself, and be a fellow learner who has the initiative to get you all going.

3. Be sure everyone knows that you are not there to interpret one another's dreams but to help one another learn how to ask the right questions so that the dreamer is in charge of the interpretation.

4. Charge members five or ten dollars a session, and require that the first four to eight weeks be paid for before the beginning of the first meeting. You can use the money to buy food for the group, to buy learning materials (tapes, videos, books), or to buy consultations with professionals who visit your group in person or by speaker-phone to get you going and keep you all motivated in the early stages. Groups tend to disintegrate if people do not to have to pay in advance. You can decide upon a refund policy that seems fair.

5. Meet for about two hours once a week if possible (once a month will do if your schedule is too busy for weekly meetings). I think it works best to assign one dreamer per week and have the others practice being interviewers in turn during the meeting. This usually gives one dreamer enough time to work through a whole dream and, more importantly, gives everyone a chance to develop interviewing skills.

6. Be careful to respect the dreamer's authority over her own dream. Discourage anyone who gets pushy or intrusive. Protect the dreamer

from having her dream overworked. Let her stop whenever she has
had enough.

7. Keep an air of lightness to the group. If someone gets into areas
that are deeply troubling, consider getting a consultation from a
psychologist. If you keep this a study rather than a therapy group,
you will be more likely to thrive over time.

8. Encourage one another to keep reading, listening to tapes, and
attending lectures and workshops so that each member can enrich
the group.

However you map out your explorations of dreaming, I
hope this information will encourage you to stick with it
until you master the ability to understand what you are
saying to yourself each night. Life is so much fuller when
you include your dreams.

Remember that each person's dreams are custom-made.
Any one-size-fits-all interpretation won't really fit anyone
well. If you want an interpretation that follows the con-
tours of your life, that makes sense, and that brings you
insight relevant to your particular circumstances, honor
the personal nature of your dream images and the feelings
that surround them. As you gain skill in dream interviewing, you will be delighted to see how exactly your dream
fits you.

Good luck to you. And may you have both sweet and
tangy slumbers.

Notes

Chapter One

1. Artemidorus, *The Interpretation of Dreams* (Park Ridge, NJ: Noyes Press, 1975), 31–33.
2. Anne Faraday, *The Dream Game* (New York: Harper & Row, 1974), 6.
3. ———. *Dream Game,* 84–85.
4. Karen Signell, *Dreams: The Wisdom of the Heart* (New York: Bantam Books, 1990), 167.
5. Artemidorus, *Interpretation of Dreams,* 60, 61.
6. Leon L. Altman, M.D., *The Dream in Psychoanalysis,* rev. ed. (New York: International Universities Press, 1975), 215–16.
7. Artemidorus, *Interpretation of Dreams,* 129.
8. Sigmund Freud, *The Interpretation of Dreams* (New York: Avon Books, 1966), 390.
9. Freud, *Interpretation of Dreams,* 276.
10. Alexander Grinstein, *Freud's Rules of Dream Interpretations* (New York: International Universities Press, 1984), 243, 244.
11. Artemidorus, *Interpretation of Dreams,* 107.
12. Freud, *Interpretation of Dreams,* 394–95.
13. Freud, quoted by Grinstein, *Freud's Rules,* 285.
14. Ilan Kutz, *Dreamland Companion: A Bedside Diary and Guide to Dream Interpretation* (Los Angeles: Hyperion, 1993).
15. Artemidorus, *Interpretation of Dreams,* 132–33.
16. Friedrich Nietzsche, *Beyond Good and Evil,* trans. Walter Kaufman (New York: Random House, 1989).
17. Artemidorus, *Interpretation of Dreams,* 133.

Chapter Two

1. Karen Signell, *Dreams: The Wisdom of the Heart* (New York: Bantam Books, 1990), 24.
2. *Guida all'interpretazione dei sogni* (Milan: Giovanni De Vecchi Editore, 1995), 312.
3. James Fosshage and Clemens Loew, *Dream Interpretation: A Comparative Study,* rev. ed. (New York: PMA Publishing, 1987), 26.

Chapter Four

1. Karen Signell, *Dreams: The Wisdom of the Heart* (New York: Bantam Books, 1990), 37.
2. ———. *Dreams*, 238.
3. Raymond De Becker, *The Understanding of Dreams and Their Influence on Man* (New York: Bell Publishing, 1978), 136.
4. ———. *Dreams*, 214.
5. Carl Jung, *Dreams*, Bollingen Series 20 (Princeton, NJ: Princeton Univ. Press, 1974), 131, 218.
6. Signell, *Dreams*, 69.
7. Sigmund Freud, quoted in Alexander Grinstein, *Freud's Rules of Dream Interpretation* (New York: International Universities Press, 1984), 92.
8. G. H. Miller, *Ten Thousand Dreams Interpreted* (New York: Rand McNally, 1978), 95.
9. Jung, *Dreams*, 275.
10. Signell, *Dreams*, 213–14.
11. ———. *Dreams*, 254.
12. Grinstein, *Freud's Rules*, 82.
13. Freud, *New Introductory Lectures on Psychoanalysis (Standard Edition 22:5–183)* (London: Hogarth Press, 1961), 24.
14. Grinstein, *Freud's Rules*, 125.
15. Signell, *Dreams*, 212.
16. James Fosshage and Clemens Loew, *Dream Interpretation: A Comparative Study*, rev. ed. (New York: PMA Publishing, 1987), 26.
17. Jung, *Dream Analysis* (Princeton, NJ: Princeton Univ. Press, 1984), 647.
18. Medard Boss, *"I Dreamt Last Night . . ."* trans. S. Conway (New York: Gardner Press, 1977), 76.

Chapter Five

1. Loma K. Flowers and Jane Zweben, "The Dream Interview Method in Addiction Recovery: A Treatment Guide," *Journal of Substance Abuse Treatment*, vol. 13.2, 1996, 99–105.
2. S. Ellman and J. Antrobus, ed., *The Mind in Sleep* (New York: John Wiley & Sons, 1991), 308–26.

Bibliography

Altman, Leon. *The Dream In Psychoanalysis*. Rev. ed. New York: International Universities Press, 1975.

Artemidorus. *The Interpretation of Dreams*. *Oneirocritica*. Translation and commentary by Robert J. White. Park Ridge: Noyes Press, 1975.

Bonime, Walter, with Florence Bonime. *The Clinical Use of Dreams*. New York: Da Capo Press, 1982.

Boss, Medard. *"I Dreamt Last Night . . ."* Translated by S. Conway. New York: Gardner Press, 1977.

Caligor, Leopold, and Rollo May. *Dreams and Symbols*. New York: Basic Books, 1968.

De Becker, Raymond. *The Understanding of Dreams and Their Influence on Man*. New York: Bell Publishing, 1978.

Fagan, Joan, and Irma Lee Shepherd, eds. *Life Techniques in Gestalt Therapy*. New York: Harper & Row, 1970.

Faraday, Anne. *The Dream Game*. New York: Harper & Row, 1974.

———. *Dream Power*. New York: Coward, McCann & Geoghegan, 1972.

Fosshage, James, and Clemens Loew. *Dream Interpretation: A Comparative Study*. Rev. ed. New York: PMA Publishing, 1987.

Freud, Sigmund. *New Introductory Lectures on Psychoanalysis, Standard Edition vols. 15, 16*. London: Hogarth Press, 1961.

———. *The Interpretation of Dreams*. New York: Avon Books, 1966.

Grinstein, Alexander. *Freud's Rules of Dream Interpretation*. New York: International Universities Press, 1984.

Guida all'interpretazione dei sogni. Milan: Giovanni De Vecchi Editore, 1995.

Gutheil, Emil. *The Handbook of Dream Analysis*. New York: Liveright Press, 1951.

Jung, C. G., *Dreams*. Bollingen Series 20. Princeton: Princeton University Press, 1974.

Mattoon, Mary Ann. *Understanding Dreams*. Dallas: Spring Publications, 1984.

Miller, Gustavus Hindman. *Ten Thousand Dreams Interpreted*. New York: Rand McNally, 1978.

Natterson, Joseph M., ed. *The Dream in Clinical Practice*. New York: Jason Aronson, 1980.

Perls, Frederick, Ralph Hefferline, and Paul Goodman. *Gestalt Therapy*. 4th ed. New York: Julian Press, 1951.

Signell, Karen. *Dreams: The Wisdom of the Heart*. New York: Bantam Books, 1990.

Thomson, Sandra. *Cloud Nine: A Dreamer's Dictionary*. New York: Avon Books, 1994.

Index

Gayle M.V. Delaney, Ph.D.

Gayle Delaney, Ph.D., is the founding president of the international Association for the Study of Dreams and co-director with Loma K. Flowers, M.D., of the Delaney & Flowers Dream and Consultation Center in San Francisco. A graduate with highest honors from Princeton, she is the author of *The Dream Kit, Living Your Dreams, Breakthrough Dreaming, New Directions in Dream Interpretation,* and *Sensual Dreaming.* Gayle is a frequent media guest and lecturer on dreams in English, French, and Italian. Her dreams have nurtured her courage and flamboyance in tango dancing, ice skating, and regular Roman sojourns.